A YEAR AT S.

The diary of a temporary bachelor of a certain age

OTTO GODWIN

Conceived, written, designed, typed and typeset by Otto Godwin

Copyright: © OTTO GODWIN 2008

ISBN 978-1-4709-4860-3

'The customer is never wrong'

César Ritz

'If men liked shopping, they'd call it research'

Cynthina Nelms

INTRODUCTION

In autumn 2006, after many years of married and busy family life, I suddenly found myself completely on my own. My wife had left for Germany and France for the third year of her Modern Languages degree course, my son had moved to Cornwall to work in the music industry and my daughter had taken up her place at university in London. My goodness was it quiet! Now, most people keep diaries of exotic places visited and exciting people met but, sad person that I am, I decided to keep a blog of my weekly trips to the local Sainsbury's. Now here it is in book form - the diary of a temporary bachelor of a certain age wrestling with wonky trolleys, Nectar points, trying to buy British and so on. Empathise!

THANKS

My thanks go to:

My wife Sharon (who made it possible)
My son William
My daughter Victoria
Allison & Nigel (for suppers & Spooks)
Barbara & Richard (for suppers and giving me the idea)
Louise (for teas & home-made cake)

and …

All the staff at my local Sainsbury's (who never suspected!)

SATURDAY 2 SEPTEMBER – MY FUTURE'S ORANGE!

My first trip to Sainsbury's as an enforced bachelor! I am reasonably well organised – my list is in some sort of order and I attack the task with gusto. Luckily I have a £1 coin with me so I can release my trolley from captivity, although I think I need to have a 'permanent pound' in the car as I can see that in future I might not be so lucky and carrying two (or three or four) baskets round instead of a trolley would be tricky. Saturday is not the day to visit! The store is very busy and progress is slow. My goodness it's cold in the refrigerated area. You certainly need to keep moving - too long mulling over the hams and quiches could see hypothermia setting in. I note that there are 24 checkouts of which 6 are cash only/10 items or less etc and 7 to 24 are real checkouts with numbers over them. Before I leave I sketch out a plan of the first level of the car park (other shoppers eye me with suspicion) and resolve to try and park in as many different spaces as possible in the next 12 months. Sad, I know, but pioneering none the less! So, a successful visit - I can see that there is a lot that I can turn my attention to in the coming weeks. Well, not that successful as it turned out because I forgot some things! So, I have to make a quick return visit on Sunday. How very annoying, hopefully just teething troubles. Although having said that, I'm quite glad I had to come back because I notice on my Sunday bill that it says 'THINK 21 Cashier Confirmed Over 16' whereas on my Saturday bill it says 'THINK 21 Cashier Confirmed Over 18'. So can 16 and 17 year olds buy something on a Sunday that they can't buy on a Saturday? Some research needed! This time I go through the '10 items or less' lane as I only have 6 items. There is an annoying man in front of me who insists on using a credit card for a transaction for the princely sum of £3.69. Why do people do this?

Items bought 33 + 6
Cost £57.17 + £7.63
Average cost per item £1.66
Checkout number 14 + 22
Nectar Points 1084

Now this is the day and time (around 2 o'clock) to shop. The store is virtually empty and I get round in record time, albeit not much of a record after only one previous visit (ignoring the quick after-visit). Still a record is a record! Maybe I ought to time my visits and divide it by the number of items purchased which would give a buy per minute ratio? This would then be something I could genuinely compare from visit to visit to see how I am doing. Anyway, I am really well organised this time. I have my list prepared in ambulatory order - salads, then fruit, then vegetables, then the cheese & ham counter and so on. Talking of the cheese and ham counter I think this is an area that I will be reporting on a lot in future. Today there were six people behind the counter and one of the young men had realised that if he put his net hat in front of his face and held one of the big knives in front of him in a menacing manner he looked like a fencer! This was greeted with little mirth by his colleagues and even less by the waiting customers. I must watch out for more sparkling entertainment from the cheese & ham team in future! There is a big promotion on wine at the moment and a lot of it is 25% off. I guess the £8 a bottle stuff just doesn't sell these days and so slashing the price moves it along nicely. I bought a bottle of Chilean white which was reduced by 25%. At the checkout I notice that the conveyor belt that shoves all your shopping into a big pile isn't working and I ask the check out girl why not. She mumbles that she doesn't know so I vow to ask the same question every time I check out and see how long it takes to get an answer. Perhaps Health & Safety have closed them all down? On the way out the car park barrier is broken. Most people would have paid before they notice this so there is little or no incentive for the car park owner to get it repaired. Oh, I forgot to say that when I arrived I sped through the car park and drove straight into a parking place without having to follow the retards who trundle around the car park looking up every alley for a slot. On the way home, congratulating myself on an efficient shop, I realise I forgot to buy the steak for tonight's supper. Oh well, chicken it is!

Items bought 27
Cost £45.86
Average cost per item £1.70
Checkout number 13
Nectar Points 1174

FRIDAY 15 SEPTEMBER – "BELTS ON PLEASE"

A bit earlier this week so the store is quite busy with lunchtime shoppers. Must curb my excitement next week and delay the visit until after 2 o'clock. Not a particularly interesting visit, although whilst debating whether to buy a doughnut or a Belgian bun at the bread & cakes display I overheard a conversation between two girls in the bakery. One of them has a large spider on the top of her curtains which, although she is not afraid of spiders, she is clearly concerned about. It seems to have been there for a while, so long in fact she has called it Winston! Quite why she chose that name she didn't tell or maybe she did after I had grabbed a doughnut (12p, a bargain) and hurried on. Got to the checkout and asked the girl why the conveyor belt doesn't work (as I resolved I would do) to which she replied that it does and promptly turned on a switch. "Would you like it on?" she asked as my cauliflower, tomatoes, Special K and the like piled up at the end. "No thanks" I replied. So, the mystery is solved – they do work but are only turned on if customers ask. So in reality they stay turned off. I notice that the stalk with the pin number machine on has collapsed so the whole thing is a bit of a mess, I'll have to check in due course to see if it has been fixed. As I walk to my car an arriving driver sees me and stops waiting for my space. So, I deliberately slow down and take a while unloading my shopping from the trolley, taking it back to the trolley park to get my £1 back, getting in and driving off. When I finally do go there is a good queue built up and as I go round toward the exit I see lots of free spaces. Why do people do it? The car park barrier is still broken. When I get home I notice that my bill says 'Published terms and Conditions Apply'. Whatever are these? Where are they published? I will enquire about this, something to look forward to.

Items bought 45
Cost £77.65
Cost per item £1.73
Checkout number 10
Nectar Points 1328

FRIDAY 22 SEPTEMBER - NECTAR POINTLESS?

I'm in just before lunch today and it's really quiet. Think I'm getting the hang of this! A really dull shopping experience, nothing much to report. I've started looking at my bills more carefully following the 'Think Cashier' message (still not sorted). I notice that there is a Nectar points statement at the bottom. I now have 1462 points! I presume this means I can get a free bag of crisps or something. I really don't know why they bother with all this – the amount you 'earn' is so small and is it worth all the effort? Why not just give people who spend over £50 money off at the checkout? Now that would be a real incentive! Anyway I've gone back to my earlier entries and put in the Nectar points balance, not sure why, it just seems an informative thing to do. Also there is a 'Nectar Qualifying Balance' which equals the amount of my bill – I presume that some purchases don't qualify for Nectar points. What could these be I wonder? I also notice that the bill says at the bottom 'Please keep for your records'. I wonder how many people (apart from me) actually keep their bills?

Items bought 36
Cost £63.81
Cost per item £1.62
Checkout number 20
Nectar Points 1462

SATURDAY 23 SEPTEMBER - BRINGING HOME THE BACON

Yes, I'm back again. Daughter off to university tomorrow so we're doing a 'big shop' so she can eat for the next couple of weeks. Actually it's quite relaxing – I push the trolley and she does the shopping! We try and find some British unsmoked bacon (I refuse to buy Danish bacon or, worse still, bacon from the EU) but it is virtually impossible to find any. In the end we find some Duchy bacon; I presume this is the stuff Prince Charles has? I've worked out that I get 2 Nectar points for every qualifying £ spent. Yippee!

Items bought 71
Cost £117.67
Cost per item £1.65
Checkout number 16
Nectar Points 1696

Chucking it down with rain today as I get to Sainsbury's at about 2.30, a bit later than I was hoping. Anyway, today the car park ticket machine is broken so everyone parks for free. I wonder how long it has been out of service? Perhaps it has caught some disease from the barrier just behind it? I've noticed that the tarmac on the ramp up to the car parking decks is starting to come off so when cars go round the corner there is the American style squeal of tyres. Also, in the wet, there is no grip in those areas. This will test the car park owner – to repair it means shutting the car park, so I suspect this is a problem that the car park owner hopes will just go away. I'm shopping for one today and it is actually quite difficult – chops, fish, chicken etc all seem to come in packs of two and upwards, so I'm going to have to be imaginative with the freezer (or eat two portions – how greedy is that?). I was accosted by a TalkTalk rep by the bakery. Not content with phoning me at home at all hours of the day and night they now attack me whilst I'm doing my shopping. The theme music on their adverts is Thunderclap Newman's 'Something in the Air' – 'Someone in Sainsbury's' is more apt, it seems. "Can I ask you a question?" she says. A good line because most people say "Yes" and then they're hooked. I say "Yes, but I won't reply", now how cool is that? I forget to collect some soup so I have to go back, the first time my list in ambulatory order has failed! At the checkout I notice that the girl's badge says her name is Dorota. Now, being a real European, I know that all girl's names in Poland end in an 'a' (I wonder why?) so I ask if she is Polish. "Yes!" she says. I say I speak a little Polish and do a bit of practising (showing off). I forget to ask where in Poland she comes from. The bill comes to £43 for a week's shopping for one person. I allow my undergraduate daughter £40 a week in food money, so knocking off the cost of my beer from my bill, it seems that she is getting the right money. By the way, whatever did happen to Thunderclap Newman? Does anyone care? Do widzenia!

Items bought 27
Cost £43.88
Cost per item £1.62
Checkout number 11
Nectar Points 1782

First, I have to report a quality problem. The chicken I bought last Friday had a sticker on it saying 'Use by 5 Oct'. Not sure what 'use' means – the mind boggles! Anyway, I kept it in my fridge and opened it on 3 October and…….. what a terrible smell! Clearly it had gone right off and was unfit for human (or my) consumption. So it was despatched to my hungry brown friend outside the back door and Sainsbury's owe me £2.79. Interestingly I think the man in the street would say that 'Use by 5 Oct' means use by midnight on 5 October. And he would be right! 'By' is defined in the dictionary as 'Of time – not after' so the proverbial man is correct. But is that what Sainsbury's mean it to mean I wonder? Do they really mean 'Use by no later than 4 October'? If so, their labelling is wrong. Whatever, my chicken would still have been off. Anyway, on to today's visit. I had to go at lunchtime (as I had nothing for lunch) and I was expecting a huge crowd but it was surprisingly quiet. I bought a piece of 'pork and egg cutting pie' from the cheese and ham counter. The last time I bought a piece it was called 'gala pie' and in fact before that I recall it was known as 'veal, ham and egg pie'. I can understand that 'veal' is not politically correct any more and there was probably no ham in it anyway so that title had to change. But what was wrong with 'gala pie'? Nice and anonymous and not as unhealthy sounding as 'pork and egg cutting pie'. Mind you, I suspect it is somewhat unhealthy so Sainsbury's might as well be honest and call it like it is. No sign of my friend the fencer today, I wonder where all those young men went. Are they butchering behind the scenes somewhere? At the checkout the (what I will from now on call) cashier (a much better name than checkout girl, don't you think?) asked me if I wanted to have my Nectar points deducted from my bill or carried forward. "How much?" I ask. "£7.50" she replies. So, with this information I can work out how much these dreaded Nectar points are worth. So, here goes... First, 2 Nectar points are awarded for every qualifying pound spent. My balance after today's purchases is 1844 points which would have therefore cost £922. And for this huge amount of money I have earned the princely sum of £7.50, a mere 0.8%. This seems to be a waste of time – why not scrap the scheme and just knock 1% off everybody's bill at the checkout and be done with it? I'm surprised though that 1844 points equates to £7.50 because that means that every point is worth a very odd fraction of a pence -

.4067245p to be precise. This is the kind of figure that the Inland Revenue would dream up not a commercial organisation like Sainsbury's. I'll check my balance again next week – I may have misheard the cashier. The car park ticket machine and the barrier are both working this week. Hurrah! The tarmac on the ramps is getting worse though – the down side is now coming off and it won't be long before it is a skid run when it's wet. I committed the cardinal sin when I came in the car park – I actually stopped and backed up to go into a free parking space. The worm has turned …

Items bought 21
Cost £31.44
Cost per item £1.49
Checkout number 14
Nectar Points 1844

FRIDAY 13 OCTOBER – "AND THE WINNER IS …"

Have just realised it's Friday the Thirteenth. Well, nothing's happened yet, so far so good! Anyway, I had a pleasant surprise when I arrived at Sainsbury's just before lunch (no lunch again so I had to go then) - there was a big banner up saying 'Supermarket of the Year 2006'. How exciting is that! But what on earth does it mean? Did they enter or was there a team of sleuths who went round Sainsbury's, Waitrose, Tesco etc looking for 'a pleasurable customer experience', 'quality with value' and 'a partnering exemplar' and all those other phrases that mean very little to the average shopper. I will find out and report back. I wonder who came second but, more important, who came last? Despite the bannered plaudit … it happened. I got a wonky trolley. This thing had a violent twist to the left, which, although it made pushing it tough going, as my prevailing route is anti-clockwise it worked out really rather well. Had a big debate with myself about which green vegetable to buy. I know there is a well known phrase or saying, something like 'A green a day keeps your spleen at bay', and broccoli is just about as green a vegetable as there is. But it did seem expensive considering most of it is stalk. I have heard that people take in knives and cut off the stalk before buying broccoli because of this. I suspect this may be a crime – theft, fraud, grievous broccoli harm? Anyway I settled on a baby cabbage which is just right for one. I bought another chicken this week. Oh, I have taken advice from a farmer friend who said I need to take off the cling film type wrapping before putting in the fridge. Why doesn't it say this on the packaging? It was only by chance I mentioned it in passing so this problem could have persisted week in, week out and Sainsbury's would owe me considerably more than £2.79. Talking of £2.79, I noticed that **all** the small chickens weighed exactly 1.3 kilograms and cost £2.79. How can this possibly be? It sounds like the humans in the film Logan's Run who are programmed to die at 25 – perhaps these chickens are 'managed' (not 'modified' note) to die when they are a shade over 1.3 kilograms (to allow for feathers, head etc to be removed). Or maybe they are cleverly cut up but I could see no sign of any signs of this – they all had two legs, a breast, no beak etc. I do find this a bit unnerving but I'm not sure how I can investigate it further. You remember that I bought a bottle of Chilean wine that had 25% off, well today it's 50% off. Needless to say I bought a bottle. I tried to buy some baked beans but could I find them? I did eventually, under ... 'pulses'. Whatever is a pulse? Well, the answer is 'seeds of leguminous plants as food collectively'. So now you know! I asked about my Nectar points at the checkout again. The young man said I still had £7.50, but wasn't sure whether this was before after today's purchases, although he did say when I asked him why it was exactly £7.50 that he thought you get £2.50 for every 500 points. If this is true, then my balance will stay at £7.50 until I get 2000 points and then will go up to £10.00. I clearly need some tactics here – how silly it would be to cash them in now when I have 1944 points! I need to resist the temptation and wait until I have just over 2000 before taking this rash step. Clearly, I've not bottomed this out yet, so more on it in due course. At the checkout I noticed all sorts of leaflets for cheap loans, pet insurance and so on. I picked up the car insurance one – Little Bill says I can save up to £126 so it must be worth a try, but only if I can do it on line as I hate answering all those questions when you ring up for a quote. I asked at the enquiry desk to see the 'Published Terms and Conditions', as I said I would. The lady there was very helpful although thought I was completely insane (probably true). She undertook to find out and let me know in 2 weeks when she's back from her holiday. Good for her. Both car park barriers are broken this week and the tyre squeal is getting worse – it sounds like a scene from Miami Vice now. Will have a drink of my wine tonight and toast Sainsbury's success in becoming 'Supermarket of the Year 2006'. Chilean wine at half price? They get **my** vote! I've just noticed that doughnuts on my bill cost 12p but are marked at 13p in the bakery area. For once in my life I'm ahead …

Items bought 31
Cost £50.61
Cost per item £1.63
Checkout number 23
Nectar Points 1944

THURSDAY 19 OCTOBER - LITTLE BILL'S BROTHER BIG BILL

OK, I know it's Thursday but I'm away tomorrow so I have had to bring forward my weekly shop by 24 hours. And it's very quiet! Maybe I should come on a Thursday every week? I have a stinking cold so I am not at my most investigative, I'm afraid. Still, I did check out Little Bill's enticing offer of £126 off my car insurance during the week. Unfortunately Little Bill forgot to tell his brother Big over in insurance about his offer as when I had dutifully filled in all the boxes my quote came back as £135 more than my current premium! 55% more. So much for Little Bill ... I assume to actually get cheaper insurance from Little Bill you have to be 50 something, working in financial services, living on the Isle of Mull, driving a Smart for not more than 1000 miles a year and keeping it in a garage overnight. Well, I'm none of those things, but I am an average sort of person, driving an average sort of car and living in an average sort of place so I would have thought Bill could have done better. I will not be beaten though! Sainsbury's have lots of other leaflets offering yet more 'cheap' deals so I will try something else soon. Back to my shopping! I decided to buy a cake for my son's birthday. He has a nut allergy, not too bad these days, but obviously I needed to be careful. Could I find a cake either without traces of nuts or one which might not be tainted by nuts during the manufacturing process? In a word, no. I find it very surprising that all the cakes, and there were at least a dozen, were, in theory anyway, unsuitable for my son to eat. How can a jam sponge cake be possibly tainted by nuts during the manufacturing process? The only thing I can think of is that the bakery where they are made is staffed by people who are completely nuts and who spend their time tainting the cakes. Anyway, I bought one as I'm sure it will be OK. I assume Sainsbury's are so paranoic, paranoaic, parannoyic, worried about being sued they say all their cakes are risky to nut allergy sufferers just to be safe. This has to be overkill (or underkill really). I bought some more British bacon this week – on the top shelf with all the other 'adult' bacon – and, get this for a title … 'Ultimate outdoor reared unsmoked British back bacon rashers'. No wonder its packaging was so big! I have nearly cracked the Nectar points puzzle. At the till I was told again that 500 points = £2.50 off, so as my points are now just over 2000 I can get £10 off anytime I choose. But there is one final question and that is as you can deduct the value of the points every time you check out what happens if you have less than 500 points? Does the cashier ask you if you want to deduct the value of your points only to inwardly smirk as he or she deducts ... nothing?! So, a little bit more investigation to do before Nectar points are put to bed. I've noticed on my bill (not so little this week, due to the cake) that some items have a * against them. Whatever can this mean? I'm on the case ... That's about it for this week (snuffle, snuffle) but you might be interested to know that if you **are** 50 something, working in financial services, living on the Isle of Mull, driving a Smart for not more than 1000 miles a year and keeping it in a garage overnight it will cost you £139 to insure it with Sainsbury's ... unless you know better.

Items bought 24
Cost £43.92
Cost per item £1.83
Checkout number 14
Nectar Points 2030

This space deliberately left blank

OK, I know, it's Thursday again ... well, again I'm out all day tomorrow so it's another Thursday visit to Sainsbury's I'm afraid. And it is noticeably quieter than Friday, which I guess makes sense. Perhaps I'll move my shopping day to Thursday permanently? And my cold has gone, so I'm a bit more on the ball this week (but, in my case, everything's relative). Anyway, today I bought some salmon and a quiche from the Sainsbury's 'Basics' range, and, frankly, I'm worried. The packaging is all white (whatever did happen to Michael Barrymore?) and very utilitarian and it looks like it has been smuggled in from Eastern Europe in a container at the dead of night. And basic actually means … cheap! So, the question is ... is the Basics range all it's cracked up to be? I think I'm on to something here as the label on my Basics salmon says 'Salmon Fillets Different Shapes' which doesn't sound too bad (in fact I'd be more worried if they were the same shape as this implies 'management') but my (little) bill says 'Salmon Fillet Tails' ie the bum. Yuk! So I think I need to buy some more from the Basics range and see how the descriptions compare. Perhaps we are being sold a pup? Not literally, of course, but, then again, you never know ... More on this in due course. Moving on, I've found that the small chicken (still 1.3 kilograms and £2.79) is actually too big for me unless I have chicken everything for 2 or 3 days so my brown friend outside the back door is doing rather well. The chickens go large, medium & small and what I need is very small or micro – an egg perhaps? And on to what is becoming my favourite area – the checkout. I did ask for my Nectar points off this week, and everything I was told is true – I did indeed get £10 off my bill. And it is more sophisticated than I thought in that the 2000 points were deducted from my Nectar points 'account' so I don't lose any points when I cash in. Even so, next time I will ask whether I can have the money off from the points I've earned from just the one shopping trip and see what happens – my guess is that I won't be able to do it. We will see! The cashier asked whether I would like him to pack for me. This is an interesting question as to get round the store and buy from all the varying heights of shelves, fridges, deep freezes and so on you need to be able bodied with all limbs in good working order so having done all that packing is a breeze. I wonder who takes them up on their offer? Maybe I should feign exhaustedness (is this a word?) and then stand around whistling, reading the paper, chatting to the other customers etc etc. Before I left I asked about the 'Published Terms & Conditions' again and was told it had not been forgotten. I also noticed that the 'Supermarket of the Year' banner has gone, come to think of it I don't think it lasted more than a week. Clearly a week is a long time in retailing. You'll be interested to know I've checked out what Sainsbury's won and, believe it or not, they did well. At the Retail Industry Awards held at the Grosvenor House in London at the beginning of October (were salmon tails on the menu?) they won 'Supermarket of the Year' (beating Waitrose, Asda and Marks & Spencer – wot no Tesco?) and 'Fresh Produce Retailer of the Year', Julie Morton won 'Store Manager of the Year' (she runs the Hedge End branch in Southampton … is there an Arse End branch I wonder) and John King won the 'Outstanding Achievement Award'. "Whoever is John King?" I hear you ask. Well, he is Mr Sainsbury's, the big cheese, the top dog, the Chief Executive. So, whilst well done Sainsbury's, Julie and John, I have to say I'm not convinced about this kind of thing - it's all a bit nepotistic and mutual back slapping for my liking and, frankly, not particularly relevant to the likes of me and my fellow shoppers. One of the judges drooled "Sainsbury's has given us permission to enjoy food. It has made good food mainstream - you come out of Sainsbury's wanting to cook". Whatever does this mean? Looking at my fellow shoppers today I can't see them rejoicing having been given permission to enjoy food, all they want to do is to do their shopping and get home as soon as possible. Following my disappointment with Little Bill's car insurance offer last week this week I picked up the pet insurance leaflet. I don't have a pet but I'd be interested to see what can (and more interestingly what can't) be insured and how much it costs. You never know, I might buy a pet so I would like to know before buying what's the cheapest to insure – a cross between a parrot and a lion perhaps. "What's one of those called?" I hear you ask. Well, to be frank I don't know, but when it talks you bloody well listen. The old ones are the best!

Items bought 21
Cost £30.45
Cost per item £1.45
Checkout number 15
Nectar Points 90 (after the great October cash in of 2000)

Yes it's Thursday again! Well, I've got my shopping down to such a tee now that it lasts exactly a week and so in I have to go today otherwise I get no lunch. Anyway, this week I don't have a pound coin to release the trolley from captivity (it had to happen sometime) so I ask on the enquiry desk for some change. Whilst there I congratulate the enquiree (she who receives enquiries) on Sainsbury's winning the 'Supermarket of the Year' award. She looks at me blankly. "Did we?" she asks. I point to the banner just above our head (an apology is due – it was there all the time and wasn't taken down after a week after all), which she hasn't noticed. "Did you get a bonus?" I ask. Gloomy facial expression, followed by "I'm just pleased to have a job…..". So I was right – disappointingly the award means nothing when you get down to the local level. So come on, Mr King (the big cheese) get some pride & passion into your local stores and make your employees feel part of a winning team! Anyway, on to this week's shopping experience, which was actually pretty uneventful. I've noticed that the man on the wet fish counter is a younger version of Captain Birds Eye – now how appropriate is that! I wonder if Sainsbury's have done this on purpose by advertising for a wet fish counter manager who looks like an old dog. Sea, that is. Talking of dogs I checked out Sainsbury's pet insurance, and I'm afraid they only cover cats and dogs. How dull. I was hoping to be able to insure my cross between a parrot and a lion (when it talks you bloody well listen) but no such luck. I found another item from the Sainsbury's Basics range today – 16 Seafood Sticks. They look like small pieces of seaside rock (can you still buy this?) and they so took my eye I bought a packet (a bit racy at 89p but it is in the interests of research). Their description is 'Individually wrapped crab flavoured surimi fish protein sticks with water and starch'. Goodness, that sounds awful. And even worse it says 'Thailand' on the packaging. So, whatever is this stuff? Well, contrary to what you might think surimi is actually not a fish but is 'minced, processed fish used in the preparation of imitation seafood, especially imitation shellfish'. A sort of mash of all sorts of fish which is then flavoured, in this case with extract of crab. Believe it or not, it is all above board and surimi is a recognised fish product. But it looks grim and I think my purchase is likely to end up in my brown friend outside the back door (although this means opening it which I am somewhat loth to do. I wonder if my sticks have the word 'Thailand' through them like the sticks of rock of old? I was under pressure at the checkout today so forgot to ask if I could deduct my Nectar points from my bill (under 500 so it shouldn't be possible). The conveyor was on (without me asking) and it doesn't half make you pack in a rush as all this tsunami like shopping comes hurtling towards you. I only just had time to pick up a Savings leaflet; I've got a bit put by so I'll give this a go after my disappointments with car insurance and pet insurance. Next, the car park. My aim to park in as many places as possible in my Year at Sainsbury's is not going too well as on quite a few occasions I've been forced to park in the dizzy heights of Level 2. The problem with Level 2 is that to get back to it with your shopping trolley requires an escalator ride to Level 1, a lift ride to Level 3 followed by a ramp walk down to Level 2. Tough for the geographically challenged like me. OK, you've worked it out, why don't I get the lift to Level 3 and cut out one leg of the journey? Well, I always forget and do the 'walking out onto Level 1 and looking for my car like a fool' routine before realising my mistake. And I know it's getting repetitive but the exit barrier is still broken. Finally, I've noticed that in addition to 'mature cheddar', 'small chicken' and so on my bill I managed to make some surprising purchases – I like the sound of Lorraine Quiche (a French tart, no doubt) and Warburton Crusty (a character from Little Britain?). There must be a name for this kind of thing, they're not spoonerisms (those are Shirley Bassey = Burly Chassis) or malapropisms (like Del Boy's "good to be back on the old terracotta") but something similar. Any ideas? Anyhow, must go, I'm eager to try my individually wrapped crab flavoured … (not).

Items bought 31
Cost £51.03
Cost per item £1.65
Checkout number 11
Nectar Points 192

This one too …

Well, I managed to last for 8 days and I am now back into my Friday lunchtime routine. So, what happened today? I'll guess I'll start with my old friends the Basics. I bought some Basics toilet rolls and whilst I surmise that basic means simply cheap, frankly with toilet rolls I'm not that bothered. They look as though they have less sheets (or whatever the technical term is, shits perhaps?) and are less wide than Andrex and the like but they look OK to me and I'm sure will do the job (actually I will do the job and then them….). I did do a bit more investigating of the Basics range and there are quite a few canned vegetables in the Basics range – tomatoes, peas, baked beans (yes, I now know these are pulses but they're near enough a vegetable as to make no difference). As I presume these are simply other brands with utility labels, I tried to compare the style of the tin that Basics tomatoes are in with the other brands of tomatoes to see if I could see any similarities. Well there were some - same size, same number of concentric rings etc but nothing conclusive. Maybe I'll buy some other Basics and their equivalent 'real' brands and compare the products? Then again, perhaps not. One thing I did notice was that there are tinned potatoes in the Basics range. Tinned potatoes! Whatever next? Whilst in the (real) vegetable area I had to pick up a wodge of those small plastic bags that you put your vegetables in as they had tumbled onto the floor. And they are quite heavy! So, each individual bag has some weight, albeit small, and this has got me thinking as to how the weighing and pricing all works. For example, my chicken (small, still 1.3kg and £2.79) is priced at £2.15 per kilogram so it should cost me £2.795 to buy it but I am only charged £2.79. So Sainsbury's have lost 0.5p. Hurrah! I wonder if this 'rounding down' is normal? Anyway, my carrots weighed 0.455kg and are priced at £0.69 per kilogram, so this works out to 31.39p and I was charged 31p. Fair enough. But doing the same sum with my potatoes (are you still with me?), this worked out at £1.2753 and I was charged £1.28. Also fair enough, I think. Anyway, what it means is that 0.5p and below is rounded down and above 0.5p is rounded up. I wonder if there is any law or practice (correct spelling, note) on this sort of thing? I don't think there is a regulator for the retail industry (Offshop perhaps) but Sainsbury's could always round the exact 0.5p up rather than down. Now there's a thought - I bet all those pennies would net them a tidy sum and nobody really could complain (or even notice). I asked to have my Nectar points deducted at the checkout and the cashier said I didn't have any. Untrue, I think what she meant was that I had less than 500 and therefore had not reached a cashing-in point. Which is what I thought would happen. So, I think that wraps up Nectar points, although I did notice I can get them on my electricity bill, but it's such a palaver (there's a good old word you don't hear very often these days) I'm not going to bother. I parked on the hugely high Level 4 today (I have given up my aim of parking in as many spaces on level 1 as possible as I just can't seem to find one most weeks, disappointing but there you go). No oxygen supplied but I did notice that the décor in the corridor is like new – clearly few people get up this far! OK, not particularly interesting, I know, but 'interest' leads me neatly on to the Sainsbury's Savings offer which I have checked out. It says 'Think Big. Up to 4.60%* AER' but on delving into the small print on the bottom of the last page I find that the * means an investment of £100,000 and above is needed! I have to say what I have put by is a bit short of this HUGE amount. And AER is defined but again not until the small print on the last page and anyway is virtually impossible to understand. I think it basically means you get less than you think you will. Maybe it should be LTYT instead? But the real killer is that the blurb explains that the Sainsbury's rate is higher than the average of several hundred other similar accounts. So, the slogan on the front of the leaflet shouldn't be 'Think Big', but 'Think Just Above Average – That's Us!'. Not a vote winner, I admit, but nearer the mark. So, three Sainsbury's offers down (car insurance, pet insurance and savings) and not many left to go. Next week, I'll be checking out their loan offer, I think I know what my conclusion will be. Finally, I had another Lorraine Quiche on my bill today (French tart, you'll remember) and a Roll Poppy (lucky Poppy and something for me to look forward to). Sad person that I am, I bought a country granary loaf hoping for an inappropriate abbreviation on my bill but it wasn't to be …

Items bought 28
Cost £44.22
Cost per item £1.57
Checkout number 16
Nectar Points 280

OK here I am back in my usual Friday slot, raring to go! So, what happened today? Well, not very much it has to be said. I think I'll start with my friends the Basics (again). This week I discovered Basics yoghurts. I was sorely tempted, I have to admit, particularly when I noticed that it said 'Still with real fruit' on the packaging. Sounds great, but the use of the word 'still' seems to imply that this satisfactory state of affairs is not going to last and that real fruit is destined to be dropped at some stage in the future in favour of … what? Fruit flavouring? The fruit equivalent of surimi (remember that from a few weeks ago? And yes, it is still in my fridge unopened). Anyway, having been tempted I decided against them in favour of some 'pork and egg cutting pie' (the pie formerly known as 'gala pie' and even more formerly known as 'veal ham and egg pie'). And, guess what? The name has changed again to ... 'pork cutting pie'. I asked the lady behind the counter (should I say lady or woman, I can never remember) if the egg was still in it and she picked up both chunks (not quite sure what the correct name for a thick slab of this stuff is) and peered carefully at each end to find no sign of any egg. So what is on sale now is just good old pork pie! I wonder who thinks up all this name changing and ingredient altering stuff and to what purpose? Well, whatever the reason, it is now off my shopping list – no egg, no buy (isn't that a Bob Marley song?) I'm afraid. I decided to buy some English wine this week as I am keen to buy British when I can (even though it can sometimes be really difficult – witness my bacon buying in recent weeks). So, I walked slowly up and down the wine displays looking for English wine (particularly on the top shelf with all the adult wines) but couldn't find any even in the area for the also rans (Blue Nun, Piat d'Or etc etc). So I asked a stocker upper (he who ups the stock when it is running low) and was told that they used to do two. And then he did the walking slowly up and down the wine displays routine as well, but to no avail. We concluded that it was no more, presumably it sold poorly and Sainsbury's axed it. I'm very disappointed. English wine is good stuff these days so come on Sainsbury's – you are a British company and should be supporting British producers as much as possible. So, get some in, run a 50% promotion and do some end of aisle displays. That should do the trick. Here's a promise - if you stock it, I'll buy it. And I'm sure all the other readers of this diary are up for it as well! Aren't you both? Now, on to bags. I've gone green! Despite the message on the Sainsbury bags at the checkout 'Please re-use', I have to admit that my only re-use is for rubbish prior to them being put in my large black friend outside the front door. I read an alarming statistic that, if I remember correctly, some 10,000 plastic bags are given away by supermarkets every minute in Britain and all of them take forever (literally) to bio-degrade or whatever the technical term is. So, I've unearthed two green (appropriate colour) bags that have a piece of plastic inside to give them shape and I used these today at the checkout – result ... no Sainsbury's bags were needed! One small step for man ... However, why ever don't Sainsbury's take a lead and charge for the plastic bags and use the money raised to fund research into recycling? And don't charge 1p or something derisory, charge 10p per bag as the aim must be to significantly reduce the usage of these eco-unfriendly things. Alternatively turn to recycled brown paper bags (I think they have these in the USA) - even ones that could be used in my brown friend outside the back door (there's another idea, two in a week!). I know it's not a big selling point – 'come to us and be charged for bags' is not a brilliant slogan (sounds like one for a brothel) – but my goodness it certainly makes a statement about Sainsbury's greenness! Anyway, that's about it for this week, I haven't had time to check out the Sainsbury's loan offerings yet, but it's in hand and I'll report back next week. Just had a look at my bill, another Lorraine Quiche I'm afraid (I'm a sucker for French tarts (not sure I should say that but I think you know what I mean)) and a new member of the cast – O Lemon Cookies. This sounds like a song title like 'Oh Shenandoah' or 'O Sole Mio' or even the famous American football star O L Cookies' real name. Or am I thinking of somebody else perhaps?

Items bought 32
Cost £52.89
Cost per item £1.65
Checkout number 19
Nectar Points 384

THURSDAY 23 NOVEMBER - LOAN MOAN

Well it had to happen sometime. No, I haven't been asked to take over running the show from Mr King or running anything else for that matter. Yes, you've guessed it … the Christmas decorations are up!!! Well, it's nearly the end of November so I guess that's not too bad. I seem to remember not so long ago television adverts for The Famous Grouse, Woolies, Boots and other brands that only seem to wake up at Christmas used to start almost straight after the August Bank Holiday weekend. But, although I don't watch a lot of television, I haven't seen too many this year (yet), thank goodness. And whilst the decorations are up at least the carols haven't started yet so the excitement is being phased this year! Today I found a trolley that had somehow escaped from the rest of the herd (or whatever the collective name for trolleys is – a basket perhaps?) so I didn't need a £1 to release it. Not quite sure how this would have happened other than the trolley rounder upper (he who rounds up the trolleys) set one free by accident. I found it with all the other trolleys though so obviously freedom was not all it was cracked up to be and now it was pining for company, a mate etc. Anyway, now for some good news! The pork and egg cutting pie has not been superseded by the pork cutting pie! Both are now being sold – how exciting is that!! And for the same price per kilo, so obviously I bought the one with the egg as the egg is free. Eggsellent. Whilst at the ham and cheese counter I noticed an old looking poster for a brand of country farmhouse cheese saying 'Ask for some today'. So I did – and, blow me, they actually had some which rather took the wind from my sails as I was expecting the server (she who serves) to deny all knowledge. Now, I have to admit I lied last week. When I said I looked at buying the Basics yoghurts and decided against them, I did actually buy some. I found them at the back of my fridge today, so I will try them. I had a very lively cashier this week. Instead of turning the inbound conveyor on and off, he stood up and leaned down the conveyor and picked up my cauliflower, pork & egg cutting pie, Special K etc. Maybe he's been told he needs more exercise and this is a way of getting some? I've noticed that none of the cashiers put your credit/debit card into the sockety thing on a stalk that you put your pin number into. Instead they do a very theatrical swiping at the side of their till. So, ever the rebel, today I stuck my card into the sockety thing but the lively cashier took it out saying it didn't work. Why not? Seems odd. I will persevere! Mr Lively also gave me a petrol voucher. I've never had one of these before (why not?) and they look a good deal – 5p off per litre which is around 5%. Mind you, I've no idea where the nearest Sainsbury's petrol station is so if I'm not careful I will fall into the 'costing more to get there than you save' trap. But it was nice to get a voucher, even so. It must be Christmas! As I will need some extra funds for my Christmas shopping I've checked out the Sainsbury's loan offer and guess what? In theory, anyway, it looks OK. The leaflet says you can borrow at '6.5% APR typical'. I've never really understood APR, only that I suspect it means it costs you more than you think, and the 47 (yes, 47) lines of small print on the back page don't offer any explanation. I do know, however, that 'typical' means sort of an average and the actual rate you are quoted when you apply will vary depending on your credit history and so on. Anyway, inside the leaflet Sainsbury's compare their rate and repayment amounts with other big hitting lenders such as NatWest, Egg and so on and (surprise, surprise) they are the cheapest. Of course, what they probably have done is to just list those lenders that charge more than they do so it's not surprising they're the cheapest. If you go to their source, Moneyfacts, there you will find rates better than Sainsbury's. But, having said that it does seem that the Sainsbury's rate is pretty good, so, after my disappointments with car insurance, pet insurance and savings, this is very welcome. Interestingly, after the 47 lines of small print (and it is really small – electron microscopes needed) it says 'Information is available in large print on request', so I'm tempted to ring in and ask for all the small print stuff to be sent to me in large print and stand by for a huge thud as this wad of paper hits the doormat. Anyway, next week I'm checking out Home Insurance where the leaflet is tempting me with a saving of up to £107 ... Ha! We will see. Well, that's about it for this week, the car park exit barrier was broken again (I saw it not working when I came in) and I gleefully watched as people put their money into the cash machines unaware that they could park for free. Now, how nasty is that? Still, it is over a month to Christmas and my festive spirit, goodwill to all men etc has yet to kick in.

Items bought 35
Cost £60.99
Cost per item £1.74
Checkout number 12
Nectar Points 504

Well I saw something today that I've never seen before. As I was going into the car park there was a man with a handful of chips. "So what?" I hear you ask. But this was a momentous sighting – to find out why you will have to hang in until the end of this week's entry. And then there was another rare site – an outgoing customer about to return his trolley to the herd (and in the store rather than in the car park). Quick as a flash I offered him £1 which he accepted. So, no need to have to shove the coin in the slot and then wrestle with the chainy thing that always seems to get caught in the trolley as you decouple it from its mate. To be fair, I have actually done this before and I remember once getting caught out because when I came to return the trolley and recover my £1, guess what? No £1. One of those escapees from the herd I was talking about a few weeks ago. So before I 'did the deal' as the saying goes I had a quick look to make sure his slot was filled (not sure I should say that but you know what I mean ...). So, what was in store in the store for me today? Frankly, not much and I was in a BIG rush so my usual sharp eye spent more time looking at the clock (I don't wear a watch) than for gems from Mr King's world for my diary. Anyway I did buy very green bananas today which go by the title of 'home ripen' rather than the more apt 'much too soon to be picked'. I wonder if Sainsbury's actually order unripe bananas or whether they come in with all the other bananas and rather than reject them Sainsbury's have thought up a neat name so they can sell them as normal? And I wonder if they are cheaper than yellow bananas? I hope so as I bet Sainsbury's pay little or nothing for them. So, I looked back over my bills (neatly 'kept for my records') and most of the time I buy 'Bananas Loose' at 85p per kilo, although sometimes I am charged by the bunch 'Bananas x 5' or 'Bananas x 6' and once, God help me, I bought some 'Basics Bananas'. Whatever were these I wonder? Anyway, as I'm a bit short of news, I think I will take stock as to what I am currently investigating and where it's all got to. This will be helpful to new readers of my diary who can't be bothered to go back to the beginning and read all the early stuff. So, here goes ... - 1) I've investigated Nectar points and I now understand how they work but I remain to be convinced all the messing about is worth it for the less than 1% 'cashback' I get from my purchases; 2) I'm still waiting to see the 'Published Terms and Conditions' as I bet these are gripping read;

3) I haven't investigated the 'Think 21' and 'Think 18' entries that appear on my bill; 4) Neither have I investigated the items marked with a * on my bill; 5) I've checked out a number of Sainsbury's leaflets offering 'cheap this' and 'better that' and most (all?) are pretty grim. Currently I'm checking out the Home Insurance offer and will report next week; 6) I'm worried about the 'Basics' range and have started to look at this; and 7) last but not least I've noticed that all the small chickens weigh exactly 1.3 kilograms week in, week out which I find unnerving. Anyway, the moment you have been waiting for has arrived … the man with a handful of chips. Well he was actually mending the car park machine! He had circuit boards, wires and other electronic wizardry all over his lap and, amazingly, he fixed it whilst I was doing my shopping and the exit barrier was in fine working order when I left. Just a couple of closing things – remember Lorraine Quiche and Warburton Crusty on my bill? This week I had a Pain Rustique which sounds like something you get in the lower back when you dig the garden. And, horror of horrors, this afternoon I was doing a bit of spring cleaning at home (a bit late I know, or for those of you whose cups are always half full, a little early) and I found empty boxes with the dreaded 'orange and white smuggled in from Eastern Europe in the dead of night' look which contained a 'Basics' toaster and a 'Basics' kettle. Whenever (and whoever) bought these? And where are they now …………..? Finally finally, for the lottery lovers amongst you to date I have gone through the following checkouts – 10, 11 (twice), 12, 13, 14 (three times), 15 (twice), 16 (twice), 19, 20, 22 and 23. You'll remember that there are 18 real checkouts from 7 to 24 (the other 6 are cash only/10 items or less) and I've been through 11 of them in 16 weeks so there are only 8 to go (I've resolved to have gone through them all in my Year at Sainsbury's). Not bad, huh?

Items bought 22
Cost £41.05
Cost per item £1.86 (higher as I bought a DVD for my daughter's birthday)
Checkout number 15
Nectar Points 586

Well I uncovered some surprising bananial (the adjective of banana) facts this week. Remember the green bananas I bought last week and my conclusion that they would be dead cheap because Sainsbury's probably paid very little for them? Wrong! There they were again this week being sold in a pack of 5 for 99p with no clue of their price per kilogram on the packaging (I thought that all food had to have this on the label?). So, I weighed them and found they were 0.7 kilograms. Doing the math means that they cost £1.41 per kilogram. This is hugely more expensive than loose bananas at 85p per kilogram (loose meaning they have become debunched) and Basics bananas which come in at 78p per kilogram. How can this be? Why should we have to pay more for the pleasure of watching them turn from green to yellow in the comfort of our own homes? Whatever, it's the Basics for me from now on (despite my wariness of Basics I really can't see what can be wrong with Basics bananas, unless you know different). I asked again for English wine today on the principle that if I ask for it often enough the wine stocker upper (he who stocks up the wine) will get a message to the manager who will get a message to the regional manager and so on up to Mr King that there is a real demand for it and stock it they will. Bit of a long shot I know but worth a try. He said no it was no longer stocked but then was incredibly knowledgeable about which wines were good value etc etc and I took his advice and bought a New Zealand something or other (which was good!). I have checked out the home insurance and … oh dear. First, the programme crashed right at the end of the answering of questions bit just as I was about to push the 'Get Premium' button. Ever persistent I tried again but the same thing happened. Up came one of those messages that are unintelligible unless you speak Icelandic, you know the ones with the little red circle in the top left corner. This one said 'R6025 – Pure Virtual Function Call. Runtime Error'. Of course! I thought of that as soon as it happened. But, hold on, this must have been caused by Sainsbury's, a good job it wasn't serious otherwise it could have resulted in a claim. Whatever, this is not good, I know my wife's computer is 5 years old but I'm surprised this could have happened. Come on Sainsbury's please get this sorted. So, on to my computer (we are multi-computer family) to try again. Now, my computer is a real cracker. My old one was forever old and, last year, looking at the Dell catalogue (I suspect the only person ever to have done this) I saw one labelled as an ideal starter computer with a picture of two youngsters looking lovingly at the screen. All for £250 including VAT (for once they actually included VAT in the price quoted) and delivery (but excluding youngsters). So I bought one and ... it's great! Anyway, this time I put in some realistic amounts for valuables and expensive single items and the like and kept getting a 'You must ring us, we cannot do this online' sort of message. So I bring these amounts steadily downwards until they are accepted, push the 'Get Premium' button and, somewhat inevitably, the amount is much more expensive than I'm currently paying for much higher levels of cover. So, thumbs down I'm afraid. Next week, life insurance (which could be tricky as I am 'of a certain age' albeit in good health). Now, the asterisks on the bill. These are simply items which include VAT! There is a surprising range of stuff that includes VAT – wine, crisps, calendar (next year's, I am thinking ahead) and even fruit juice. I did a bit of research and crisps are not regarded as food (how true!) and hence attract VAT, calendars are stationery not books (which are VAT free), wine you can understand as the Government is hell bent on grabbing as much tax as possible but fruit juice?? I wondered it if it was a mistake and so sent an e-mail to Tropicana who indeed confirmed that fruit juice like fizzy drinks and the like attracts VAT. Completely bizarre. Why not make it VAT free and hence cheaper and hence more attractive than the unhealthy fizzy drinks? Why not, indeed. Next, the 'Published Terms & Conditions Apply' message at the bottom of the bill. Very uninteresting – all it means is that if there are guarantees, warranties etc given on any item (for example, electrical goods) then they apply! I parked in bay 279 this week in the car park. This is the furthest space from the entrance on the dizzy heights of level 5 (or was it 6?). Can't remember, must have been altitude sickness. Felt a sense of pride as I assume I have boldly gone where none have gone before but nearly got blown away as it was bloody windy up there in the jet stream.

Items bought 24
Cost £44.28
Cost per item £1.84 (higher as I bought a book)
Checkout number 18
Nectar Points 674

Things are looking up! Today there was a big swanky Bentley in the car park. Perhaps it was John King on a royal visit or maybe someone's chauffeur noticed both the ingress and egress barriers were out of action? When my year is finished maybe I should calculate the % of times that I would have parked for free because the barrier was not working had I not had the 'spend more than £15 at Sainsbury's and park for free' pass. If you see what I mean ... Well, what goes round comes round. The TalkTalk representative was there again and asked me the same question as before – "Do you mind if I ask you a question?" but, this time, before I could reply coolly "No, but I won't reply" she asked me two questions. I guess there might have been a remote possibility that I was interested in TalkTalk but not when she asked "Do you collect Nectar points" as her opening gambit. This was followed quickly by "Do you have a BT landline?". I mumbled "No" to both questions and hurried on. The prospect of being bogged down with Nectar points from someone other than Sainsbury's fills me with horror – one bee (nectar provider) is enough! Now, salmon. I know there is a big hoo-hah about farmed salmon, something about it being dangerous and it does look spectacularly pink, but I buy it nonetheless. I nearly got caught out, though, this week as lurking within the salmon display was salmon farmed in ... Norway. And, needless to say, it's cheaper than Scottish farmed salmon, so if you buy the cheapest without reading the labels you end up with salmon from Norway. Norwegian farmed salmon is probably only a small step away from surimi, you remember - the somewhat questionable mushy stuff that I bought a few weeks ago in the interests of research, which ended up in my brown friend outside the back door. Anyway, celebrations are in order today – Sainsbury's have won another award! This time they've won the 'Wine Supermarket of the Year' (despite not selling wine from their own country – good job I wasn't a judge). I have to say this comes as a real surprise. OK, they have lots of the stuff but are they really any better than any other supermarket? The Sainsbury's website says that their recent focus has been to 'improve the shopability of the wine aisle'. Whatever does that mean? In my local store it's the same width and length as it always has been with bottles on shelves and some special offer stickers (which this week referred to wines that weren't there – shopinability presumably). Maybe I will check if 'shopability' is in the dictionary – I suspect it's some marketing speak which is completely over the head of mere mortals like me! Also the website says that 85 new wines have been introduced. How can that possibly be? The shelves are the same length and height so it can only mean one thing … some lines have been dropped. Aha! Perhaps that's what happened to their English wine. The judges were 'particularly impressed by high level of training Sainsbury's gives its collegues (sic – you will be!) in the wine department and … the information offered to customers'. Well, whilst training is very laudable what benefit do I, the customer, get from this? The only evidence I've seen is the stocker upper (he who stocks up) is very helpful and seems to know his grapes from his onions but I bet he hasn't had any of this 'high level of training'. And what 'information?'. This implies there are helpful little write ups on each wine saying things like 'excellent with cold meats and cheese' or 'complements surimi' (note I have spelt 'complements' correctly, although perhaps it should be 'spelled'?) but there aren't! So it seems that what the judges 'found' is not borne out by the reality at the local store level. Anyway, on to the checkout. Today my cashier started talking to himself! I asked if he was OK, to which he replied that he was not staying on after 2pm which is when his shift ended as he wouldn't be paid any extra and blah blah blah. I sympathised with him but strangely he has little pride in working for a company that has been voted 'Supermarket of the Year' and 'Wine Supermarket of the Year'. And, of course, on reflection, I don't think Mr King could have been visiting today in his swanky Bentley as if he had my cashiering friend would have been falling over himself to stay on late. But then again perhaps not!

Items bought 31
Cost £53.80
Cost per item £1.73
Checkout number 14
Nectar Points 780

And this one …

Well, the Christmas shopping list has arrived by e-mail from 'la femme' in mainland Europe and I am attacking it with gusto. The main problem, however, is I have no idea where some of this stuff is in the store and therefore I am suffering from severe disorientation. For example, I cannot for the life of me find panacota, pannaccotta, pan ... little bits of bacon, so I ask a most helpful assistant who troops around the store with me and he asks another assistant and all three of us troop around the store and eventually find them … all sold out. Of course, it didn't help that what I was looking for was actually pancetta! Whatever, despite my intention that all my Christmas shopping will be done in one visit to the table (as they say on the snooker programmes) it looks like I'll be back again later in the week. I have to say this takes the pressure off as I'm not sure about some of the items on the list (incorrect purchasing will not be tolerated) and will need to refer to Ms Lister for guidance and clarification. I am, however, proud of being able to track down rubber gloves (don't ask). Having searched in vain I finally spot an unsavoury item removal operative (cleaner) wearing some rather fetching examples and she points me with her rubber finger (again, don't ask) in the right direction. On going into to Sainsbury's this time there is a huge banner over the door offering Bernard Matthews' turkeys at half price! Now, there's a tempting offer. Boooooootifull, in fact. Now, Matthews' whole turkeys may be okay but I thought his turkey products are reconstituted from left over bits of bird? And presumably, therefore, he has to collect complete kits of parts (breast, skin, glue etc) with which he then builds his turkey products? And, I guess that, as they're pretty grim, they don't sell well and this must have rubbed off on to his whole turkeys - so out come the banners advertising them at half price. I think I'll pass if you don't mind Bernard. I have to ask on the enquiry desk for £1 to pay the ransom to get my trolley released and the enquiree (he who receives enquiries) proudly announces that I am the fourth person that day (it's around 4pm) who has asked a similar question! Nice that there is someone else who remembers completely useless information like this - a man after my own heart. Sainsbury's is quite festive today, the carols are in full swing as you go in and the assistants have decorated themselves with tinsel, red fleeces, those funny reindeer ear type things you stick on top of your head etc etc. They have also set up a lectern at a strategic position in view of the checkouts manned by a young lady who is ensuring that everything works like clockwork – and, good for her, it does as the queues are not too bad at all. The good thing about Christmas for me is that most of the checkouts are open so with a bit of luck I can go through one that is normally closed, thereby crossing another number off my list! Anyway, back soon … (as those annoying little stickers on shop doors say, the lying hounds).

Items bought 52
Cost £75.13
Cost per item £1.44
Checkout number 23
Nectar Points 930

THURSDAY 21 DECEMBER – A MERRY XMAS TO ALL MY READER

My problems are solved! She who writes the lists is now back for Christmas and today we are in Sainsbury's doing the last 'Big Shop' together before the Big Day. And there are more than 3 days to go so we are well ahead of ourselves. No last minute Christmas Eve panic buying for Mr & Mrs Organised! And it goes like clockwork. The puzzling items on the previously e-mailed list are easily dealt with and acquired, the pancettas are back in stock (I buy 4 to celebrate) and all the unlisted items that are de rigeur (French) at Christmas such as clementines, stuffing, gammon, aluminium foil etc are gleefully swept into the (large) trolley. And my wife pays the bill (but only after cashing in (stealing) 500 of my points). And to cap it all both the ingress and egress barriers on the car park are broken so everyone parks for free at Christmas. There is a God! One of the good things for me about buying unusual items is that the till roll or whatever it's called reveals yet more interesting purchases. 'Olde English Chest Stuff', for example. This sounds like a cure for pneumonia sold by a vendor off the back of a cart in the 1700s (no lorries then). And then there's a 'Colgate Pump'. This could well be a stomach pump for those of you who bought the Bernard Matthews' half price turkeys! Or to deal with a dicky Olde English Chest perhaps?

Interestingly aluminium foil comes up as turkey foil on the till roll –presumably calling it aluminium foil is politically and environmentally incorrect these days? I must remember to put it in the recycling. Talking of remembering I just remembered I saw a Sainsbury's lorry on the motorway recently … in the Basics livery! I tried to see if it had an Eastern European number plate but the rain and spray made this impossible. OK, that's it, back again after the festivities are over. Happy Christmas!

Items bought 111
Cost £222.55 (huge)
Cost per item £2.00
Checkout number 22
Nectar Points 874 (after the spousal theft of 500 points)

SUNDAY 24 DECEMBER – "ONCE, TWICE, THREE TIMES IN SAINSBURY'S …"

Damn. Back again on Christmas Eve. We actually ran out of some things before the great day. So I'm back for some speed shopping (a bit like speed dating, but with a trolley). And I'm in and out in record time. And as I got it all in a basket (just) I was able to go through one of the 'Baskets Only' checkouts (another one off the list!). But then … disaster. No Nectar card. I think my wife kept it after the great theft of points on 21 December and so as my bill says 'Using a Nectar card today would have earned 52 Nectar points' this has cost me 25p. Oh well. Happy Christmas (again and for the last time hopefully).

Items bought 13
Cost £26.12
Cost per item £2.00
Checkout number 6
Nectar Points 874 (same as last time)

Another one…

Oh dear. I've made a terrible mistake. For some bizarre reason I thought that Sainsbury's Chief Executive's first name was John. But it isn't. It's Justin. King. So all my diary entries referring to John King are completely wrong! Whilst this is probably high treason, luckily treason (along with piracy with violence) ceased to be a capital (hanging) offence in 1998 so I will live to tell the tale (which I am doing). I've thought about going back and changing all my entries but I've decided against it. But now I know why he didn't send me a Christmas card. Anyway, what's done is done. Please accept my apologies Mr King. The good news is that I've checked out Sainsbury's life assurance offer over the Christmas break. After the excitement of opening my present (sic) I needed something inane to do. I decided against getting a quote as such life insurance I have was put in place many years ago (I am of a certain age) and to compare it with a quote today wouldn't be a fair comparison. So, instead, I got a quote for a 34 year old non-smoking woman (one not on fire presumably) for £50,000 of level cover for a 15 year term. "Why?", I hear you ask. Well, it's the example in the Sainsbury's leaflet. And guess what? The Sainsbury's website wouldn't give me a quote as the monthly premium would be less than £5 which is very odd as the leaflet says the monthly premium would be … £5. So, I steadily increased the sum insured (or is it assured?) until it would quote me to find that the non-smoking etc woman could actually get £63,065 of cover for a £5 monthly premium, ie a better deal than the £5 per month in the leaflet! I'm not sure what to make of this – it's good that the leaflet is prudent but it's somewhat alarming that it's wrong. Perhaps in the time since the leaflet was printed Sainsbury's have decided to look more kindly on 34 year old non-smoking women? But the date on the back of the leaflet (under the small print – only 5 lines this time) is for last month and surely life assurance rates can't have changed that much in only a few weeks or so? Maybe Mr King's wife fits the bill (little) and so some subtle changes have been made to get her a better deal??? 'Every little helps' as the saying goes +… Anyway, on to this week's shop. First flour. OK, not my usual purchase I have to admit but it's on the list so must be bought. And, bravely, I buy Basics flour because the slogan on the bag reads 'A little less refined. Still rises to the occasion.' and I feel some affinity to this statement being a bit rough myself and still being able to rise to the occasion (sometimes). The mince pies are half price this week – I wonder if they will get even cheaper as the weeks go by? Or will they just disappear from the shelves? Something to look out for as I'm not worried about eating mince pies in April and by then they could be really cheap. The pork and egg cutting pie (remember this?) is also half price so, gleefully, I buy a chunk. Talking of eggs, amidst the barn eggs, free range eggs etc are eggs from … France! Now I've nothing against our French friends but is it really necessary for Sainsbury's to buy in eggs from France – surely we have enough production in Britain to satisfy demand? It certainly looked like it from the egg area in the store. I went completely mad this week and bought a medium chicken for £2.99 and, yes, you guessed it, they are all £2.99. Can anyone explain how all the small and medium chickens can be exactly the same weight and same price? Sadly, there was one solitary turkey for sale, nearing its sell by date and looking a little miserable. And not even a Bernard Matthews one! I suspect it will never be sold now and will have to go into Sainsbury's brown friend outside their back door. Finally, I nearly got bonked in the car park (I thought my Christmas wish had come true). Someone was doing the 'backing up to get into a car parking space' routine and didn't see me coming up behind. Luckily I have quick reactions and was able to get into reverse before my front was re-arranged. Just as well, as the offending vehicle was one of those foreign, noisy exhaust and wing on boot types driven by … you know what I mean. Talking of the car park one of the signs reads 'No vehicle can leave the car park without putting their ticket into the paystation'. What dreadful English! First, as 'vehicle' is single 'their' should be 'its' (without an apostrophe) but as vehicles cannot put tickets into machines, whilst the statement would then be grammatically correct, it would be complete nonsense. So, I suggest a good old plain English statement like 'You cannot leave the car park unless you have put your ticket into the paystation'. Or perhaps 'Pay, hoot and leave'?

Items bought 40
Cost £52.22
Cost per item £1.30
Checkout number 18
Nectar Points 874 (still - have yet to reclaim my card from thieving wife)

WEDNESDAY 3 JANUARY – UNDERWEAR NIGHTMARE

A very embarrassing shopping trip today. Many, many years ago I bought some underpants in a Malaysian street market for the princely sum of the ringgitt (Malaysian currency) equivalent of 80p for 3 pairs (I remember haggling him down from £1.20, how cool is that). Anyway, I've worn these things day in day out but, sadly, after all these years they are, in a word, knackered. I do have other pairs to wear though! I'm a bit behind with the washing what with Xmas, hungry hoards, parties etc etc so I had to don a pair of the Malaysians today. And, very embarrassingly, the elastic waste band gave up the ghost whilst I was in Sainsbury's so I had this bulge around my nether regions that looked as though I had just passed one of Bernard Matthews' turkeys. Anyway, I had to abandon my shopping trip half way round and repair to the gents to remove the offending article meaning that for the rest of the trip I went commanche style (I think that's what it's called). How very daring. My Malaysians have obviously come to the end of their useful life so sadly they will need to go but how on earth do I dispose of them in an environmentally friendly way? Is there a bin for this kind of thing at the local recycling centre (formerly known as the tip) and, if there is, what colour do you think it will be? Don't answer ... Anyway, coping with all this drama meant that my usual observations are thin on the ground this week (like my Malaysian pants after I had de-donned them). I did notice, however, that the mince pies are still going strong at 50% off. I'll give them another week before I leap in and grab a bargain. On the way out the lady in front of me at the car park barrier couldn't get her ticket to work and so she pushed the button marked 'Push' and amazingly someone answered. After much chat and more unsuccessful putting in of ticket the barrier went up – presumably the man in the machine has a golden ticket? I wonder where he is? I don't recall seeing a mission control anywhere so perhaps he is up at Head Office? Or maybe the whole thing is now 'outsourced' and he's sitting at home reading the paper? Before I go I must tell you about another great item on my bill this week – 'Swede Loose'. Lock up your daughters!

Items bought 33
Cost £51.76
Cost per item £1.56
Checkout number 15
Nectar Points 874 (still the same, this is costing me a fortune!)

FRIDAY 12 JANUARY – OFF MY TROLLEY?

At last! Back to my old routine of a Friday shop. It's been a while since I've been in on a Friday and I'd forgotten how busy it is at lunchtime. Actually the aisles were OK, but the checkouts were … well, more of them later. And, before you ask, my pants are in good order this week so last week's 'shop till they drop' problems have not recurred. But, notwithstanding this, I had a bit of a panic attack on the way in – no money and so no way of releasing a trolley from its mates. And, whilst carrying a basket has the attraction of being able to go through a checkout I've not been through before the prospect of lugging a heavier and heavier basket round Sainsbury's is not good news. So, I have to go on safari to find a trolley that has been sent to Coventry (or wherever trolleys get sent) by its chums and, amazingly, I find one. Not lurking in a dark corner, no, at the top of the escalator where I literally walk straight into it. How lucky was that! So, suitably armed I start to shop and almost immediately run into my first beef of the year - potatoes. Hithertofore I've bought Sainsbury's loose baking potatoes (the big buggers near the floor). But as I have an awful sneaking feeling that they are really expensive (I'll run some checks next time to prove this) I tried to buy some normal loose potatoes. But, guess what - they don't sell any. So, I had to buy a made up bag which I don't like doing because as sure as eggs is eggs (or perhaps spuds is spuds) you pay more for the cost of cleaning them and bagging them up. I know loose potatoes are muddy, mucky things but come on Sainsbury's get some in – we can take it! Next, mince pies. My bluff has been called – whatever stocks there were have been removed. Damn! Mind you, they did have some 'Mince Puffs' in Christmassy boxes but, frankly, I didn't like the sound of them … Neither did anybody else it seems as the stack was beautifully symmetrical and clearly untouched. What strikes me as odd, however, is I don't recall seeing these before Christmas (they would have surely caught my eye with a name like that) so how come they are on sale now? Maybe Sainsbury's are stocking up for next Christmas already? I'll keep an eye on them in the coming weeks – my guess is that the whole lot will suddenly disappear. Now, here's something really interesting. What I thought was my plain ordinary trolley is in fact a 'MK1 70 LTR Daily Shopper'! Over Christmas, sad person that I am, I did a bit of roaming around on the internet and found a company called Clares that makes supermarket trolleys (someone has to). And looking through their product range (I thought I might buy one at the end of my year as a souvenir) I came across the MK1 70 etc which looked remarkably like my friends at Sainsbury's. And Clares count Sainsbury's amongst their customers! So, today I compared my trolley with a picture of a MK1 70 etc (other customers eyed me with suspicion) and it's exactly the same apart from a sticky up raised bit at the top of the flap that goes up when they mate (I presume there is a technical term for this – answers on a postcard please). And it's an impressive bit of kit with a 'round nose', 'travelator castors' and 'electroplated zinc with clear passivation & lacquer coated finish'. Wow. I will treat my trolleys (sorry MK1 70 etc) with much more respect in future … Right, on to the checkouts. Today the checker outer was called Putin or something like that and he had real trouble with his equipment (scales, moving belt etc) and then he ran out of £1 coins so the upshot was that I had my longest ever checkout experience. Bring back the pre-Christmas girl with the lectern I say! Whilst waiting I had another look at the Sainsbury's amazing offers (not) leaflets and I noted that there are two left for me to have a go at, sorry, critically appraise – credit cards and travel insurance. Well, I don't do credit cards really (lucky me) so I'll pass on that one and as I'm not planning to go anywhere exciting just yet (unless Swindon counts) I don't need to check out the travel insurance offer. Something to look forward to later in the year perhaps? Finally, I noticed some big banners announcing 'The Big Five Drive' which is something to do with the 5 vegetables a day that we are all supposed to eat (baked beans don't count – they're pulses). Unfortunately I saw this too late to be able to do any investigating but, as luck would have it, as I returned to my car I saw a discarded scratch card type thing on the floor in the Big 5 green (naturally) livery so I picked it up. The (very) small print on the back says that every customer who spends more than £10 should be given one gamecard when they check out. You then tear it open in a frenzy of excitement to be told either, like this one, 'Sorry you haven't won this time' or, presumably, something like 'Congratulations you have won this time', in which it case it seems you hand the winning card to the cashier and then you get one of your vegetable purchases free! It was disappointing that Putin didn't give me a card (his mind was elsewhere understandably) but I'm looking forward to getting one of these every week. What isn't clear is how it all works, because presumably you have to go through the checkout to confirm you have spent over £10 and then, if you've won, presumably you have to rummage amongst your packed up shopping and compare it with the till roll so as to be able to locate the most expensive vegetable bought and presumably then the cashier has to do some kind of refund transaction which presumably means a manager authorisation and then presumably you are handed the princely sum of 47p! I predict a riot … And, much more interesting, how is this all dealt with in the Nectar points statement? Don't go there … Wish me luck!

Items bought 27
Cost £46.74
Cost per item £1.73
Checkout number 11
Nectar Points 1006 (back in business again, but should only be 976?)

FRIDAY 19 JANUARY - NO CLAIM GAME … SHAME!

Well, uncontrollable excitement today as I will spend over £10 and hence will get my first game card in 'The Big Five Drive' vegetable/fruit etc promotion. More of this later! What first? Ah yes, potatoes. Now, as I said I would last week, this week I did some potato price comparisons with some startling results. I always thought that the loose baking potatoes (bakers) were expensive and, my goodness me, they are. Bakers come in at £1.19 per kilogram as compared to King Edwards (perhaps technically there should be an apostrophe between the 'd' and the 's'? One for Lynne Truss to answer) at 63.6p per kilogram and Sainsbury's multi-purpose (the mind boggles) potatoes at 47.6p per kilogram. So, over twice as much for the pleasure of having slightly bigger potatoes. And looking at the potatoes in the Sainsbury's multi-purpose bags they, like the bakers, have been washed and there are a few that aren't that much smaller than the bakers. As the saying goes size isn't everything (I should know) so it's the multi-purpose ones for me in future. Anyway on to the hinged pine boxes. "What?", I hear you ask. Yes, the hinged pine boxes stacked up by the Indian ready meals. Goodness only knows where these have come from but there is a huge stack of them and at 25% off they are hard to resist. I've never seen these before so I can only assume that they have been imported from a larger store in the hope that they will sell. Well, nice as they are, I just don't see too many of them shifting even though they are well made (I checked) and have that nice woody smell when you open them. They remind me of the exhibit at the Tate Modern some time ago which was just stacks of white boxes so rather than trying to sell them at 25% off perhaps Sainsbury's would do better by entering them for the Turner Prize. It seems that anything that isn't art qualifies so they would be in with a shout of winning it I'm sure and then, when they have won it, they can sell them to Charles (or is it Maurice) Saatchi or some other philanth, phillann, rich bugger for a huge sum. OK, you've waited long enough, it's time to reveal that I did indeed get a game card and … didn't win. How disappointing was that? I asked the cashier if anybody ever won and he said that that 1 in 2 people win. So, by the law of averages, next week I will win. I asked him what happens when you do win and he said that you have to take your card over to the enquiry desk for validation and then you come back to the checkout and then … by this time I was losing the will to live. I have to say I'm having mixed feelings about winning now. Whilst it would be nice to get some free sprouts it sounds like it is a real mission to go through the claiming process. Anyway, as I'm bound to win soon I will find out! Now, here's an interesting one. On the way in to the car park there is a sign that reads 'Welcome to your Sainsbury's'. Interesting, but technically incorrect. Sainsbury's is actually owned by its shareholders so really the sign is only true if you are a shareholder. So, not wishing to be left out I have decided to buy some Sainsbury's shares. I'll get on to my stockbroker next week. Sorry, typing error. I'll get on to **a** stockbroker next week and buy a few. Not too many as I'm sure as soon as I buy some the price will plummet! I'll keep you posted. Finally I noticed that the Life Insurance leaflet has been reprinted with 'Sale 5% Online Discount' on the front so presumably it's not a big seller (I hope I'm not to blame). I picked one up out of idle curiosity and noticed that the '34 year old non smoking woman' in the previous leaflet has turned into a '34 year old non smoking man' in this leaflet! The figures are the same as before though (£5 per month for £50,000 of level term cover for a 15 year term). I wonder if they are still wrong? Not my problem, see you next week!

Items bought 25
Cost £38.57
Cost per item £1.54
Checkout number 16
Nectar Points 1082 (I feel an encashment coming on)

FRIDAY 26 JANUARY – "NEIGHBOURS, EVERYBODY NEEDS GOOD NEIGHBOURS ... "

I've been very neighbourly this week. One of my neighbours is very unwell so I called to see if I could do any shopping. Answer yes, but I needed a lesson in ricotta (what it is, where it would be etc) as I have to admit it is not something I have bought before. And then, coincidences of coincidences, whilst I was at the ham and cheese counter (buying a piece of pork & cutting pie, hurrah!) I hear the two ladies behind the counter talking about a senior citizen who gets a taxi to and from Sainsbury's and who walks with a stick following a knee operation and lives in my road etc etc. Another of my neighbours! So when I got back I gave her a call and what had happened was that she had put an egg on to boil and then ... gone to Sainsbury's! When she got back it was cooked (it exploded actually) but no damage was done other than bits of egg and shell all over the kitchen. Reminds me of the time when my parents came to stay, put the pressure cooker to boil and ... went out for the day. Luckily I can vouch for the fact that the little valve type thing in the lid does actually work. But the cooker was ruined and had to be despatched to the great kitchen in the sky (Heaven's Kitchen, as opposed to Hell's Kitchen which is where that swearing cook comes from). Anyway, on to this week's shop. First, the wooden boxes. They've been moved! Obviously this has been done in an attempt to garner some interest but the pile looks just as big as it did last week. And, yes, you guessed it, I counted them. There are 41. I'll keep an eye on these in the coming weeks and let you know how the sales are going. Just in passing I noted that the mince puffs (remember them from just after Christmas?) don't seem to be selling too well (not surprising really with a name like that) and putting them next to Love Cakes can't be helping … Now, on to the checkout. The lady in front of me in the queue got a 'Big Five Drive' game card and, of course, I was willing her to lose, as, if as the cashier said last week 1 in 2 people win then if she loses … the chances are that I should win. And, yes, she lost, so, with trembling hands and a beating heart (must have been the Muscadet last night) I tear open the card to find I have … not won. I ask the cashier if anybody ever wins, "Oh yes" she says "lots do". Hmmm. I saw Mr J King (note the new respect after the shameful getting his name wrong episode from a few weeks back) on television last night. He was not explaining away why the Sainsbury's pension fund had a £250 million black hole in it and what he was doing about it and why a Sainsbury's cashier on £12,000 a year would retire with a pension of only £1,500 a year. Of course, now I have resolved to become a Sainsbury's shareholder this kind of financial stuff is of interest to me – knowing my luck as soon as I invest Mr King will pledge to fill the pension fund hole in full the very next day, wiping billions off the value of the company (and my modest investment with it). He seems a nice enough guy, though, (very young looking, like policemen) and they said he visits one store a week. Come on down Mr King, I'll take you round and introduce you to my old friends Lorraine Quiche and Warburton Crusty following which we can take a light lunch (men in his elevated position would 'take' lunch, don't you think?) of pork & egg cutting pie. I'll get some in. Finally, you will be pleased to hear that I am the (temporary) proud owner of £20 of Sainsbury's gift vouchers! What a dull and unimaginative present you will be thinking but actually they were sent to me (my wife actually) as compensation for poor service. It's a long story involving daughter at university and wife organising Sainsbury's Online to deliver a birthday treat of sprouts, low fat muesli, organic orange juice … No, just kidding, it was wine, instant Indian meals, the usual student fare but, whatever, after first arriving early (a problem, as daughter, being in a secure hall, had to be there to greet it and obviously wasn't) and then it never arriving at the re-arranged time and then it never arriving at all. A complete cock up. So, in went a complaint letter and back came lots of excuses, resolutions to do things better, thanks for highlighting areas of weakness in the system etc etc all the usual stuff and £20 of gift vouchers. So these will get sent off to daughter and happiness will be restored. There is a God!

Items bought 29
Cost £35.23
Cost per item £1.21
Checkout number 13 (no wonder I didn't win!)
Nectar Points 1152

THURSDAY 1 FEBRUARY - PARKING & BARKING

Great excitement in the car park today! As I was going in there was an Enterprise rent-a-van going out through the in. Now, when you go in the in you go in on the outside but after you've gone in the in you have to go from the outside into the inside and as the van was too tall to go into the inside from the outside he had to turn round and go back out the in. And to guide him out was a smartly dressed young man with a walkie talkie (are they still called this?) who was somewhat vertically challenged. Not only all of this but also there was much consternation in the queue for the exit barrier as someone had skidded and I think run into the car in front. So, another smartly dressed young man with a walkie talkie was getting some grief from a Jaguar driver. Now what have I been saying about the deteriorating road surface for the last few months? Remember, you heard (read) it here first! I feel a letter or a phone call to the car park owners coming on. Phew - after all this drama and trauma shopping in Sainsbury's was bound to be a bit of a let down but actually there was quite a bit going on this week. First, the boxes. Gone. As I predicted, they presumably didn't sell and they've been sent to the great sawmill in the sky. But, ever entrepreneurial, Sainsbury's have replaced them with ... a pile of duvets! Wherever is all this stuff coming from? Eastern Europe, perhaps, with the Basics deliveries? Next, Sainsbury's is going the dogs. No, not really, in fact dogs are going to Sainsbury's - there was a man with a rucksack with a tiny dog (not sure of the breed) peeking out of it. Very cute, but surely only guide dogs are allowed in the store? Luckily it didn't bark otherwise goodness only knows what would have happened. One for the Health & Safety boys, I feel. Much mirth at the cheese & ham counter today. A customer's mobile phone rang, nothing unusual about that but it had the 'diddle dee dee dee, diddle dee dee dee, diddle dee dee deeeee' ring tone (the one you hear most often and the most annoying) but the phone's battery must have been nearly out of charge as the key, pitch or whatever got slower and lower as the tune progressed. It sounded really good – "I want **that** one" as Andy from Little Britain says! Now, prawns. I decided to buy some to go with my avocado (my weekly treat). I decided against the 'Basics' as they looked a little undernourished and instead alighted on some large juicy looking ones which I was dismayed to read had been 'cultivated in Indonesia, Ecuador, Honduras or Nicaragua'. Good grief! Talk about Sainsbury's hedging their bets. Why not just say 'from anywhere other than the UK' and be done with it? Not sure about them being 'cultivated' either, this has a 'modified' ring to it don't you think? And as Indonesia and the Central American countries are on opposite sides of the world where do all these prawns meet up prior to being packed for Sainsbury's? The little known country of Crustacea presumably. Whilst in the checkout queue I noticed a new leaflet, this time advertising Sainsbury's Energy. I had no idea that Sainsbury's were buying and selling gas and electricity (can anybody do this I wonder?) but, needless to say, I picked up a copy of the leaflet. I was expecting the usual comparisons with other suppliers but I was misstaken! Instead Sainsbury's simply say that not only will 'you will enjoy competitive energy prices' but also 'you could earn up to 6200 Nectar points in the first year' and this is followed by a complicated table which shows how you could indeed earn up to 6200 Nectar points in the first year. Now, as you now know 500 Nectar points are equivalent to £2.50, so 6200 points will save you the princely sum of £31.00. But, having said that, £31.00 is £31.00 so perhaps I will check out the offering in more detail. I still haven't bought my shares in Sainsbury's yet and, my goodness, I should have done as they went up by 13% today! Some talk of Sainsbury's being bought for their prime locations (alas, not the one I shop in unfortunately) but, of course, the real reason is that having learned about my intention to invest all my readers have piled in to the stock thereby forcing up the price. Fame at last! Well, that's just about it for this week apart from to report that I yet again didn't win a prize in 'The Big 5 Drive'. So much for every other person winning – that's 3 times I've not won.

Items bought 33
Cost £47.84
Cost per item £1.44
Checkout number 16
Nectar Points 246 (1000 cashed in for an 'Instant Reward' as it says on my bill.
Sounds interesting!)

FRIDAY 9 FEBRUARY – BERNARD MATTHEWS TURKEYS – THEY'RE FLOOTIFUL!

Spooky. First I say I'm going to buy some Sainsbury's shares (still not done) and the share price jumps. Then, I give Bernard Matthews a bit of a hard time and ... well you know what's happened. Whatever next? These kinds of things come in threes so as sure as eggs is eggs something or someone I mention will have good or bad news within a week or so! Well, what about Bernard Matthews then? The latest news is that he lied about bringing in birds from his 'processing plant' (whatever is that?) in flu ridden Hungary. If that's true (that he lied) then I'm afraid that he deserves whatever dire consequences comes his way as a result. It sounds very much like foot & mouth which as I recall was spread by one trader who trucked infected sheep around the country (is it really necessary to cart animals round the country like this?). And it looks like its happening again - bird flu being spread by one trader trucking turkeys around Europe. When will we ever learn? Not 'boooootiful' but 'flooooootiful'! Anyway, enough of that and on to the much more interesting tale of my weekly shop, which actually was pretty dull. First, the duvets (you'll remember these have taken over from the wooden boxes which have gone to the great sawmill in the sky). Well, they're still here and it looks like very few, if any, have sold as the pile is still pretty impressive. The down has not gone down! I can't see them still being there next week, I'm afraid. Next, pains. Pains? Yes, 'petit pains' which I think is French for small rolls (this reminds me, I once heard a French girl try to say 'wholemeal rolls' - great sport, if you know somebody French give it a go). Anyway Sainsbury's bake them in store and sell them in 2s and 4s. They look very nice and the French name on the label gives them a little more 'je ne sais quoi' but the problem is they always seem to be stale! I have bought them in the past to find the next day, even though still in date, they have turned into 'petit rochers' and have to be fed to my brown friend outside the back door. So, tempting as they were I bought some rolls with poppy seeds on instead. Are they really poppy seeds I wonder or is this just shopspeak for black bits? OK, on to my prawns which this week were 'Caught in the North West or North East Atlantic Ocean'. I think Sainsbury's are warming to my advice to just label them as 'From anywhere other than the UK' and being done with it. Something that warmed my heart today happened during my lamb chops purchasing decision-making process. As I was thrusting aside the New Zealand lamb (God only knows the food miles involved in bringing lamb all the way from New Zealand) I came across some Welsh lamb chops. OK, nothing too unusual in that but on the pack there was a photograph of one of Sainsbury's lamb suppliers, in this case David Williams from Powys. He looks like a decent, honest and hardworking individual and the Welsh name, ruddy face, 5 bar gate and grassy slope behind all added to the heartwarmingness of it all. Great! At the checkout I felt like a real regular customer as I now recognise and am on monosyllabic speaking terms with a few of the cashiers. I haven't progressed beyond "I'll manage" when asked if I want help packing but in another few weeks the queue behind me will be miles long as I chat to Danuta, Mikela, Bronsk, Stronk etc about the weather, Nectar points, Basics and the like. But this was tempered by the fact that 'The Big 5 Drive' is no more! It only lasted from 10 January until 6 February and not having won I never got the chance to find out what happened to the lucky winners. How disappointing. Oh well, you can't win them all (any).

Items bought 31
Cost £43.86
Average cost per item £1.41
Checkout number 17
Nectar Points 332

A bit late writing my diary this (last) week – it's all been a bit busy as Mrs G returned from Germany last Saturday for a brief visit and I didn't have much time post-shopping & pre-return to do my stuff. Anyway here it is at last and apologies to all my reader (sic) who has been waiting expectantly. So, what news from the orangery? Well, not much really. The duvets have gone (told you) but have been replaced by … sets of wicker trunks! These are not swimsuits previously owned by a television presenter but are essentially storage boxes. And they come in sets – you open the big one to find 2 smaller ones inside and then you open those … and so on. A bit like those Russian dolls that go on and on and on until you're left with an atom sized doll and a queue of steadily decreasing sized dolls hundreds of miles long. It does seem that my Sainsbury's (technically not correct but that's what the sign says) seems to be becoming a dumping ground for unsaleable goods from other stores – pine boxes, duvets, wicker trunks – whatever next? I have to admit to showing my age today. Whilst buying my pork and egg cutting pie I noticed that the server (he who serves) was looking leeringly over my shoulder. Interested, I turned round and, yes you guessed it, there was a smart young lady walking by wheeling her MK1 70 LTR Daily Shopper (trolley). "Not bad" I said (the girl, not the trolley). He gave me a knowing look ("I know your type"), smirked and carried on cutting my pie. I must get out more. Anyway, on to the toilet rolls. Had a bit of a running out (of rolls, not a bodily malfunction) so needed to stock up and I bought some toilet rolls which proudly state that they have been recycled. From what? I dread to think. Now, chicken korma. I usually buy a Sainsbury's chicken korma to have on a Friday night with a tin of lager and, indeed, I did buy one this week. As you know I am a keen label watcher and I always try to buy British food. I have been previously happy with buying Sainsbury's chicken korma as it says 'produced in the UK'. But as I was packing it away after I got home I noticed on the side of the packet in small print it said 'Produced using Thai or Brazilian chickens'. Oh my word! I dread to think what Brazilian and Thai chicken farms are like – they have to be a whole lot worse than Bernard Matthews (and we know what he's been up to). Why ever does Sainsbury's have to use chickens from Brazil and Thailand? What's wrong with our own chickens, for goodness sake? And maybe the Thai chickens are in fact … not chicken? I think you know I mean. Anyway, that's the last time I buy

Sainsbury's chicken korma. And, why isn't the packaging labelled properly? It should say 'Produced in the UK using Brazilian and Thai chickens' all in one go and no hiding the chicken source (sauce?) in the small print. To my mind all this recommended daily intake, calories this and vitamin that kind of mumbo jumbo stuff that nobody reads or understands should be dropped in favour of complete, clear and no-nonsense labelling about where the food actually comes from. Allied to this I noticed at the checkout that Sainsbury's are introducing a 'Wheel of Health' labelling system. This is a kind of traffic light system whereby the good bits get greens in the wheel, less good (calories) get oranges and bad bits (salt, fat etc) get reds. Hopefully this is a step in the right direction!

Items bought 33
Cost £46.45
Average cost per item £1.40
Checkout number 9
Nectar Points 424

SUNDAY 18 FEBRUARY - NO BILL (LITTLE OR OTHERWISE)

Had to have an emergency shop today. Mrs G is back from Germany and after the "Why is there no food in the house?" and "Whatever have you been eating while I've been away?" kind of supportive remarks clearly a Sunday morning visit to Sainsbury's was an absolute must. To be honest I was expecting it so took it all in good heart. Actually, Sunday morning is a good time for shopping, very quiet and not at all unpleasant (notice the double negative rather than the positive). And, whilst we bought some unusual (for me) things it was all rather uneventful so I'm afraid this is going to be a very short entry. And, disappointingly, I have lost the bill so not all of the usual mathematical stuff is at the end I'm afraid. Oh well, never mind - normal service will be resumed next time.

Nectar Points 200 (next week's balance minus last week's balance – are you with me?)
Cost £100ish (200 Nectar points divided by 2 – I'm getting the hang of this!)

An interesting week this week. My list has been enhanced by the returned one so I had to find some items that I wouldn't usually buy which took me to areas where no man had boldly not gone before (Captain's log …). The first item of difficulty was redcurrant jelly. This required a real hunt – I tramped back and forth (breaking the anti-clockwise trolley code) looking in the obvious places like 'jams and spreads' but in the end sought assistance from an orange fleeced shelf stacker upper. "Aisle 10" she said without a moment's hesitation. Impressed, I returned to Aisle 10 to find … no redcurrant jelly. I find it in the end in Aisle 9 lurking amongst sauces. Oh well, now I know for next time. I also had to buy some dressed crab in its shell, much easier as there they were in the fish counter manned by the Captain Birds Eye lookalike. Whilst he was weighing and packing I made a point of looking at the price ticket which said that the crabs had been caught in the North West Atlantic (or was it the North East? No matter) but when he gave me the package it said 'Dressed Cromer Crab'. Now, as you know, I am somewhat geographically challenged but as far as I recall Cromer is in Norfolk which cannot by any stretch of the imagination be said to be in the North Atlantic (West or otherwise). So is this more misleading food labelling? Talking of misleading food labelling, I took a closer look at the ready-made meals this week after my experience with the Sainsbury's chicken korma, the chickens for which come from Brazil and/or Thailand. Along the bit where the price tickets go there was a banner saying 'British … British … British' in a fetching purple colour (nice and regal). Encouraged, I pick up the 'Lamb in a Pot' to find that the lamb is from … New Zealand and the pork (??!!) is British. Undeterred I look at the 'Shepherd's Pie' to find that, yes you guessed it, the lamb is again from New Zealand. Of course each pack had 'Produced in the UK' on it which may be 'acceptable' but a banner with 'British' all over is just not cricket! Anyway, moving on … the wicker trunks have gone (I assume not sold) and have been replaced by bowls & side plates! These are 'free' when you buy 5 items with 'Enjoy a night in' stickers on them. This must be a new Sainsbury's promotion. God knows who thinks all this stuff up – why is it all so complicated? Whilst mulling this over I had a disaster. My glasses fell to pieces – the little screw thing that keeps one of the lenses in had come unscrewed so I had lens, frames, screw etc all over the place. I collected it all up and being an enterprising fellow I looked for a screwdriver equivalent on the shelves to effect a temporary repair. My first idea was to use a nail file – one of those metal ones with a pointed end - but, of course, these were in acres of packaging and completely inaccessible. In the end I happened upon a potato peeler with a pointed end which did the trick! I caused a bit of a queue in the checkout today. I stick the car park ticket in my mouth when I drive into the car park and leave it there until I'm in the store so, as you can understand, it gets a bit wet. Anyway, I must have overdone it this week as it wouldn't go in the little machines Sainsbury's have to let the ticket know you have spent more than £15 so you can park for free. So there was much squeezing, smoothing, shoving and pushing and in the end in it went, much to the relief of the queue behind me. Luckily the lectern was out again today so no doubt the lady manning (womanning?) it was doing a quick reshuffle of the checker outers to relieve the queue I had caused. Am I bothered? Well, 30p is 30p!

Items bought 40
Cost £57.08
Average cost per item £1.42
Checkout number 12
Nectar Points 624

SUNDAY 4 MARCH - CHECKOUT CHECK

A bit out of kilter this week. My wife has now gone to the South of France for 4 months (lucky her – sun, brie & vin) and she asked me to go out with her. So my usual weekly shop was delayed until Sunday and because she had kindly left me lots of stuff in the freezer (hopefully labelled) I only needed a quick visit to Sainsbury's. And the brevity of the visit coupled with the lack of fellow shoppers meant it was not an unpleasurable experience (note the double negative). Talking of fellow shoppers there were 2 small men with shaved heads identically dressed in grey judo style outfits doing their shopping today. I assume they are member of a religious sect but which one? Presumably one that allows shopping in supermarkets! Now, today I needed light bulbs. The light bulb area is always a mess, why should this be? I assume that customers open packets to make sure the bulbs are intact and then don't put them back properly. And of course there is a bewildering array of different shapes, colours, bayonet/screw cap, watts etc. All I wanted was an ordinary 100 watt bulb for my hall. A pretty simple request, but could I find one in all the jumble? Er, no. I got really excited at the checkout today –the young man in front of me when asked if he wanted help with his packing said "Yes"! Great, I thought, now I can see what happens and who does what. But, of course, he was joking so my hopes were dashed. But there is some good news! I have now been through all the real checkouts apart from 7, 8, 21 and 24. So, only 4 to go. Moving on, you can park for free in the car park if your stay is under 30 minutes or if you spend over £15 in Sainsbury's, in which latter case (note the elegant grammar) your ticket is validated by Sainsbury's. When you stick your ticket in the pay machine the message 'No Charge' comes up in the display. I presume there is some kind of time check to stop people sticking their ticket in the machine when they arrive and then staying for hours and hours and getting out of the car park for free. I wonder how long you're allowed to get out of the car park before your ticket expires? And then what happens? Something to ponder but not check, I feel.

Items bought 14
Cost £15.93
Average cost per item £1.14
Checkout number 9
Nectar Points 654

MONDAY 12 MARCH - IS CLAIR VOYANCE MY NEW NAME?

Oh my word. Readers will recall that I decided to buy some shares in My Sainsbury's (not yet but a little bit soon will be) and the price jumped by 13% in one day and I gave Bernard Matthews a bit of a hard time and this was shortly followed by bird flu in his factory in Norfolk. Well now it's happened again. A few weeks ago I did a bit of research into supermarket trolleys and found a company called Clares that more than likely made the trolley that I dutifully push round the store each week. I say 'made' because, wait for it, they've gone bust! How creepy is that? Is it possible that a mere mention in my diary means that something significant (good or bad) will happen to the mentionees (those who are mentioned)? Well, think it's time to

run a test. In due course I will report on a company that I come across as I trundle around the store and then see what happens. And if something good or bad does indeed happen to that company then I see a new career beckoning! Anyway, on to this week's shop which is on a Monday, I think the first time I've been in on a Monday but the day of the week is irrelevant once you're inside the hallowed portals. This week I noticed the 'Top 10 Offers' board tucked away by the fish counter. A very dull list it has to be said - 2 for 1 on this and money off that, you know the sort of thing. And, of course, it is pretty much pointless because if you do a) find it and b) read the list and c) decide to buy some of the stuff on offer the chances of actually finding it in the store are virtually nil. Of course what Sainsbury's should do is to have a big board near the entrance and then signpost (dreadful word) customers to the offers, something like 'Basics Prawns 5 for 1 aisle 7'. Maybe some 'new entries' and 'fastest movers' tags like the pop charts have (are they still called this?) would be good too. Anyway, into the toilets. I got caught short today (must be the cold snap) and visited the gents. Not the best toilet in the world it has to be said (tired, I would call it) but perfectly serviceable nonetheless. But I saw something in there I've never seen before. Now that's caught your attention! Next to the urinal was a vertical handle for holding on to. I presume this is for people who have difficulty standing but, I don't know about you male readers, but I need both hands for 'doing my business' (am I unusual?) so I don't have a spare hand for holding onto anything else, be it a handle or ...?! Anyway, being up for anything (not sure this is an appropriate phrase under the circumstances) I did try to use it but was in danger of having to emerge with two tone trousers so I had to bring my experiment to a premature close. Whatever, suitably refreshed, I continued my shopping and noticed that the plates and bowls in the 'Night In' promotion are still there and as there is still a huge pile of them presumably most customers are having nights out! This is another good example of a half-hearted promotion. To get a plate or bowl you have to buy 5 items with the 'Night In' stickers on them. But the plates and bowls are tucked out of the way and, believe me, if you can find 5 items with 'Night In' stickers you really do deserve a prize. Why not advertise the promotion near the entrance together with the (lovely) bowls and plates and with some signposting (that word again) to the eligible items? It seems to me (but not Sainsbury's local management) that this is blindingly obvious and simple, basic marketing, but there you go. Moving on, as you know I've been having a beef (almost literally) about non-British ingredients in Sainsbury's ready meals and I have vowed not to buy their chicken korma again. But, this week, I needed a ready meal so diligently went through them all until ... success! I found one made from British beef - the Beef & Ale Pie. Hurrah! And delicious it was too. Finally, on to the checkout and, yes, another one gone through (Number 7) so only 3 to go now - 8, 21 and 24. As 24 is the last of the real checkouts the chances of it being open are slim, maybe I'll get lucky at Easter time when the store will be full and all the checkouts are open to cope with the rush? Fingers crossed! Finally finally, in my trolley this week was someone else's shopping list. What an interesting find! How about 'tin tounge', 'water crest' and '1 carrott'? I must look out for these next time, I fancy a bit of tounge for my tea ...

Items bought 31
Cost £49.06
Average cost per item £1.58
Checkout number 7
Nectar Points 752

SUNDAY 18 MARCH - EIGHT ... GREAT!

Well, it's another Sunday visit again this week and, my word, the car park is empty! All those spaces I've coveted and aspired to over the weeks are free and I triumphantly park in pole position - right by the doors to the orangery. Down the escalator (not turned on, very disconcerting and disorientating), still all nice and quiet, turn the corner and ... the store is closed. It doesn't open until 11 and it's now 10.15. Bugger. So a big decision - go home again or kill time for 45 minutes. I know I'm sad but hanging around for 45 minutes waiting for Sainsbury's to open has to be the pinnacle of sadness so home it was for a cup of coffee. Returning at 11.15 what a transformation! The car park is pretty much full and the store is heaving. Clearly not the time to come. Anyway, my disappointment at being totally unable to beat the rush was tempered by some excitement on the way into the store - a man had dropped 6 bottles of wine in one of those cardboard carrier things and was glumly eyeing his St Emillion (for that is what it was) as it sloshed around on the floor. He looked so terribly sad! £30 literally down the drain. But he did have it coming, it has to be said, because the carrier was from ... Tesco! Clearly every little did not help in his (wine) case. Bypassing the wine lake (goodness red wine smells terrible at 11am on a Sunday morning) I enter the store and, continuing on the subject of wine, I notice a notice in the wine aisles proudly announcing that Sainsbury's has won the '2007 Drinks Buying Team' award. Now how about that for a job? Buying drinks for a living - your round or mine, who cares? Interestingly, though, the Sainsbury's website doesn't mention this at all, which is all a bit strange. Maybe there has been some kind of leak (appropriate for drinks buying, don't you think?) and Sainsbury's have sent round their announcements either before the award has been announced or, perish the thought, before it has even been judged. Hmmmm. Whatever, it sounds like a bit of a non-award - if indeed Sainsbury's have won the 'Drinks Buyer of the Year' and as they have already won the 'Wine Retailer of the Year' what else is there to win? How about the 'Wine Warehouser of the Year' award or the 'Moving Cases of Wine Round the Country in an Environmentally Friendly Way' award or ... well, you get my drift. Awards for awards sake? Moving on, the 'Night In' bowls & plates are still there and it would seem that very few, if any, have been given away. I can't see them being there much longer - I wonder what will happen to them when they are rounded up when the promotion finishes? I hope they go to a good home and are not just taken down to the local tip. In truth, Sainsbury's will need the room for all the Easter eggs that are starting to crowd into the store, taking over from all the Mother's Day stuff that is all over the place (today's the day, if you'd forgotten). Anyway, on to the checkout and as luck would have it row 8 (one of my last three) was open, albeit with a longish queue. As I couldn't pass up the opportunity to claim my penultimate scalp I joined the queue, despite checkout 7 having no queue (customers already in the checkout 8 queue eyed me with suspicion). As I as was waiting my turn I noticed a machine tucked away by the trolley park called a Coinstar which was proudly displaying the slogan 'Turn Coins into Cash'. I'm not sure what this machine does and the ridiculous slogan doesn't help at all – it's a bit like saying 'Turn Water into Liquid'. Whatever, the machine looks dusty and disused and it may not be here much longer so I will need to check it out quickly and let you know how you indeed can ... turn coins into cash. So, only checkouts 21 and 24 to go. 24 is the last one in the line, hopefully it will be open at Easter, otherwise I will have to write to Mr King and ask him to open it especially for me before my year is up!

Items bought 22
Cost £29.10
Average cost per item £1.32
Checkout number 8 (Yippee!)
Nectar Points 810

SUNDAY 24 MARCH – ORANGE BAG? NO ... GARBAGE!

Another first!!!!!! Yes, it's Saturday and this is the first time during my Year at Sainsbury's that I've visited the orangery on a Saturday. And whilst I thought it would be heaving actually it wasn't too bad. I met my postman on the way in. A delightful man called Ken who is always incredibly cheerful despite getting up at 4am every morning. He told me that he is in at 4.30am then spends a few hours sorting his walk (this is not putting on sensible shoes or ensuring that each pace is approximately 1 metre long but getting all the pile of post that is his round into street and house order). Then off he goes delivering it all aiming to finish about 9.30am. Not sure it's the kind of job for me – 4am is a bit early and I imagine there are more rainy days than dry ones. Talking of sorting, Sainsbury's has done some re-organisation of the store since I was last in. The vegetables and fruit area is all different and there were a good few trolley jams as people sought out their cabbages, potatoes, apples and the like. Actually it all seems very sensible – whereas before the fruit and vegetables were all muddled up now the vegetables are all in one aisle and the fruit in another. Well done Sainsbury's! Also well done Sainsbury's for some superb labelling on the packing for their white, multipurpose, tasty and versatile (the cheapest to you and me) potatoes.

Rather than the usual vague 'produced in the UK' it says 'Grown in Aberdeenshire by Phillip Benzie'. Fantastic! And an internet search reveals that Mr Benzie is a 'link farmer' for the Royal Northern Countryside Initiative and he and his link school won the 'Count and Grow with Superspud 2006' competition. So well done them. Anyway, after this heartwarming little story it's time to move on to … fish. All the salmon this week was 'Farmed in Norway' (sorry, not for me) so I bought some cod in breadcrumbs which was a 'Product of Scotland'. I wasn't sure about this as I am somewhat wary about believing any 'Produced in …' claims any more but I bought it anyway as there was nothing else closer to home on offer. I've had a look at the producer's website which was not particularly helpful (the usual 'partnering' and 'solutions' stuff) so I've e-mailed and asked them where their fish comes from. I'll let you know when (if?) they reply. Last week I noticed that Sainsbury's had won the '2007 Drinks Buying Team' award but I was a bit worried that as the news did not feature on the Sainsbury's website there might have been some kind of mistake. Well, I did a bit of research (Google) and I can confirm that Sainsbury's did indeed carry off the prize (a set of 6 cut glass wine glasses, perhaps?) at the recent OLN Drinks Retailing Awards. OLN … ? Whatever is that? Well, it's the 'Off Licence News', which presumably is a gripping publication aimed at … off licences. Sounds like a good candidate for Guest Publication on Have I Got News For You, don't you think? OK, on to the checkout (I looked to see if 24 was open, no luck I'm afraid). The first thing I noticed was that Sainsbury's shopping bags have changed from being orange on white to white on orange and they look … horrible. They also proudly announce 'This bag is made from 33% recycled material' which is hardly anything to be proud of as most of these bags end up in landfill somewhere and take zillions of years to bio-degrade. I had an overly cheerful cashier this week who chatted and whistled and scanned with gusto and then said 'toodleoo' or something like that as I left. Not having heard this word before I assumed it was Icelandic for goodbye but when I got home I checked it out and it is indeed an 'informal farewell remark'. Well, you learn something new every day (even, surprisingly, in Sainsbury's). Whilst I was waiting in line the Coinstar machine I noticed for the first time last week was being used and was making a noise that went on and on and on - just like a fruit machine delivering a huge jackpot! So, I checked it out and what you do is you chuck in a pile of coins and after it's done its stuff you get a voucher to spend in the store worth less than the value of the coins you put in (the machine takes a 'service charge', inevitably). This all seems completely pointless to me but I took a look at the Coinstar website and the whole business is based on the premise that loads of people keep loose change in jars (even me - I have to admit that I save 1p and 2p coins in a jar) and a Coinstar machine is an easy way of getting rid of them (saves you having to count them all up, put them in bags and take them to the bank, like wot I do). So, whilst the slogan 'Turns Coins into Cash' is nonsense the best I could come up with was 'Turn Coins into Sirloins' and 'Turn your Money into Honey'. OK, they need a bit of work, I know, but it's a start. Well, that's about it for this week but just in case you are wondering, Superspud is a somewhat decrepit Superman like character carrying a potato …

Items bought - 30
Cost - £43.22
Cost per item - £1.44
Checkout number – 8 (again!)
Nectar Points 896

WEDNESDAY 4 APRIL - ANYONE FOR CROQUETTE?

Yes, I know there's been a bit of a gap since my last entry (not sure I should say that ...) but I've been 'en France avec ma femme'. Anyway I got back on Tuesday to an emptyish fridge and a hungry daughter so my first chore is a trip to JS. And has absence made my heart grow fonder? In a word, no! Had to park on one of the upper levels today so took the lift down (lazy) and as the doors closed a seductive female voice said "Going down". I thought my luck was in! Anyway, the Specsavers leaflet giver outer was standing outside Sainsbury's today (Specsavers is next door) giving out, er, leaflets. Now, I always refuse this kind of thing but it's surprising how many people take a leaflet for something they are not remotely interested in. I usually say "No thanks" quite politely but the 'lady' in front of me was much more to the point and verbally attacked him with a loud "Piss Off!". The giver outer and I were somewhat taken aback by this but he took it in good heart with a smile on his face. Later I saw her muttering to herself in the store so clearly she needed more than some new specs. The bowls and dishes are gone! The 'Night In' promotion has presumably come to an end (dawn?) and so the remaining stock of bowls and dishes have been rounded up and disposed of. I wonder where they went? Very few, if any, were given out so there was quite a pile. I took another look at the 'Top 10 Offers' board today (next to the fish counter) and my eye alighted on the 'Corn Cobbettes 6 for 4' offer as a) I have never heard of a cobbette and b) whilst I've seen 3 for 2 offers before 6 for 4 seems quite bizarre. Whatever next? How about running a 17 for 13 promotion on something to get our mathematical juices really flowing? And whatever is a cobbette? Normally 'ette' is added to a word to signify 'female' or 'smaller' but as I assume corn on the cobs (or is it corns on the cob?) are sexless (but, my goodness, they look male to me) cobbettes must be small cobs which sound a whole lot better than saying ... small cobs? If adding 'ette' to the end of a word does indeed signify smallness is baguette a small bag, palette a small friend and belette a small bell? Actually belette is French for weasel so if Sainsbury's run a 'Belettes 3 for 2' promotion, be careful! Going back a bit, 'alight' is an interesting word. The only time I've heard it is on London Underground where the young lady says "Alight here for ... ". Whatever our foreign friends make of it I have no idea as I can't believe 'alight here' can possibly be in their phrase books. It does seem odd to use an expression which may be grammatically correct but rarely used in everyday speech but having said that "Get off here for ... doesn't sound particularly British does it? I do like it when she says "Alight here for the Royal Institute for the Blind" – I'll leave you to think about that. Moving on! The regal looking 'British' banner under the Indian prepared meals has gone (someone **is** reading this!) to be replaced by a banner which says 'Indian'. So far so good, but the British banner now appears under the cottage pie, bangers and mash, beef & ale pie and other 'British' prepared meals. I get it now! It's actually nothing to do with where the food comes from it's the origin of the dishes on offer. Hmmmmm. Guess what? I had a reply to my e-mail asking where the fish in the breaded cod comes from. And the answer is

... the North East Atlantic. Phew, that was lucky - I had a sneaking suspicion that by not saying where it was from on the packaging it meant it was farmed in Peru or something worse. On to the checkouts! 24 not open so no rejoicing yet but I got an Active Kids voucher this week. In truth, I've been offered them for a while but have turned them down. Now this is a really good promotion. Schools collect vouchers and then exchange them for footballs, gym equipment, sports kit and the like. I took a look at the 'shop' on the Sainsbury's website and a Slazenger Cricket Prohelmet can be had for 468 vouchers and a Mitre Tactic Football for 112 vouchers. The helmets sell for around £30 and the footballs for around £6.50 so the 'exchange rate' is around 6p per voucher. Now I got 5 vouchers for spending £50 with Sainsbury's so that's 30p worth, which doesn't sound much but if everyone was to collect them, my word, schools would be able to buy loads of stuff. The only question is ... what do I do with my vouchers? The first school to e-mail me can have them! Anyway, that's it for this week apart from to tell you that my Nectar points balance is exactly 1000. What are the chances of that happening? Who cares? Au revoir, mes belettes.

Items bought 36

Cost £52.58

Average cost per item £1.46

Checkout number 8 (like buses, you wait ages for one then three come along together)

Nectar Points 1000 (honest)

TUESDAY 10 APRIL - INDEX FIGURES

Whilst buying some bananas and other vegetables at my local greengrocer (I ran out, obviously my list making is not as good as it used to be) I asked for a bag to carry it all in and found in the bottom an old Sainsbury's bill from January 2004. With this in hand and a little investigative research at this week's trip to Sainsbury's (the Tuesday after Bank Holiday Monday - very quiet) I can produce my own SPRINTY (**S**ainsbury's **P**rice **I**ncrease **IN** **T**hree **Y**ears index). Anyway, more of that later. On the way into my Sainsbury's I noticed the banner headline on the Financial Times saying that the Sainsbury family is 'holding out'. This is all to do with the takeover bids that are floating around. I have to admit that I'm not really following it – you will remember I said I would buy some shares and just as I said this in came the bids and up went the price! So I'm a bit miffed and not following it on a point of principle. Whatever, good for the Sainsbury family! Why would they want to sell out the family business? It seems to be doing OK and as sure as eggs is eggs a new owner would no doubt make 'improvements' such as redundancies, store closures and the like and it would be a disaster if a deal was done and my local store got closed before the end of my year. So, Sainsbury family, if you're a bit short I've got a bit put by to help out (every little helps, as the saying goes ...). How about some Nectar points or Active Kids vouchers? Moving on, as I said it was very quiet today, and although I was just about the only customer one of the other customers was a man of more certain age than I am who was rabbiting on to one of the vegetable stocker uppers. On and on he went with "It wasn't like this in my day", "When I was young ... " - you know the sort of thing. The young stocker upper was clearly disinterested but, good for him, still had customer care uppermost in his mind and agreed with everything that was coming his way and just kept on smiling. As I was waiting for this little ensemble to break up so I could get to the mini cabbages I noticed that the stocker upper wasn't in fact stocking up but was about to reduce the price of ... the mini cabbages! I immediately seized on an opportunity to barter. "How much are you reducing them by?" I asked. "5p" was the reply. "How about 10p?" I asked (every little helps). "Maybe later but not now". "Are you sure?" "Yes". "Done!". Now I know 5p doesn't sound a lot but it's equivalent to a discount of 12.8% so not a bad return for the minute I spent half listening to the my fellow customer's drivel. And, if my math is right, 5p for 1 minute is £3 an hour, half the minimum wage for doing nothing! Nice work if you can get it. The store looks really uncluttered this week as all the promotional stuff has gone (plates, wooden boxes, duvets etc etc) as have the Easter eggs, chocolates, chicks etc etc. Before I bore you rigid with my SPRINTY index a little bit on the checkout experience. I was standing in a queue when the lady in front of me proudly announced that the next door man was empty. My goodness, I thought, either I'm going deaf or she has eaten too many Basics! Whatever, having looked around in vain for a skeletal male I eventually realised that what she meant was that the next checkout was clear and must have been for some time because the cashier was busy ... yawning. So, through I went and clearly he was half (or completely) asleep because not only did he not offer me cashback (a hanging offence) but also he gave me 20 Active Kids vouchers for £31.06 of expenditure. You'll be pleased (amazed) to know that I've got to grips with Active Kids vouchers much more quickly than I did with Nectar points so I can categorically say that £31.06 of purchases equates to 3 vouchers (1 voucher for each complete £10 spent) so I'm 17 vouchers up! By the way, I'm still waiting for an e-mail from a school asking me for my vouchers - I suspect that now I have 25 vouchers my inbox will be overflowing. And, I've decided to include them in my sums at the end of each diary entry. Finally, the moment you've all been waiting for - my SPRINTY index. I have to say that it was not that easy to find exactly the same products as were bought by Customer X in January 2004 and I had to give up on a good number but here's the ones I managed to find (the 2007 prices come first then the 2004 prices in brackets):

Baked beans in tomato sauce - 28p (31p) = - 10%
Tuna steaks in olive oil - 88p (79p) = + 10%
Lady Grey tea bags - 189p (159p) = + 20%
Mushrooms closed cup (.225 kg) - 52p (54p) = - 4%
Tomatoes (4.85kg) - 72p (62p) = + 16%
Bananas (.85kg) - 72p (67p) = + 7%
Semi skimmed milk - 66p (58p) = + 14%
Olivio - 228p (215p) = + 6%
Tropicana organic orange - 244p (248p) = - 0%
JS ham & pineapple pizza (yuk) - 299p (269p) = + 11%

Total - 1338p (1242p) = + 7.7%

So, my SPRINTY index shows a 7.7% increase in just over 3 years. Now, the National Statistics Office website (**very** uninteresting) shows that the All Food index was 152.6 at 16 December 2003 and 161.4 at 13 February 2007 (the latest available). The increase works out at about 0.2 per month so if I add 0.4 to the February 2007 index this takes us up to mid April 2007 (come on, keep up!) and an index of 161.8. So, the Food Index has increased by 6% over the period, compared with my SPRINTY index of 7.7%. So are

Sainsbury's ripping us off? Probably not as my index is not representative (how many men on the Clapham omnibuses (or is it omnibi?) buy Lady Grey tea?) and can only be a rule of thumb guide. I guess what it shows is that Sainsbury's increases are pretty much in line with everyone else's which is what you'd expect in such a competitive market place. And with that, I will wake you up to tell you that that's it for this week and you can go back to sleep.

Items bought 27
Cost £31.06
Average cost per item £1.15
Checkout number 13
Nectar Points 1062
Active Kids vouchers 25

FRIDAY 13 APRIL – 21 TODAY (NOT)

Another Friday the thirteenth and, as last time, nothing unlucky has happened to me today apart from having to make my second visit this week to the orangery! My daughter is still home and my son too so I am being eaten out of house and home. So, here I am again. Before I start, I forgot to mention on Tuesday that at the bottom of the 2004 bill (that I used for my SPRINTY index) there was a Petrol Discount voucher. I asked Mr Sleepy the cashier for my petrol voucher and he looked at me strangely (most people do) and said "No promotion at moment" (he is not of these shores). Frankly, after the Kids Vouchers' huge miscalculation and all the yawning I don't believe him, so next week (I forgot this week) I'm going to ask again for a petrol voucher and see what happens. Talking of promotions I took another look at the Special Offers board (still by the fish counter) only to find it was … totally obscured by a Hovis loaf cardboard container. This is not to say that Hovis loafs (or is it loaves?) are made out of cardboard (but then again …) only that there was an empty promotion (I presume) display thingy in front of the board. Based on my experience of Sainsbury's promotions thus far I cannot believe that this promotion actually worked and all the loafs (loaves) were sold, but you never know! Next, booze. I now carry round my green re-usable bags in my trolley and I bought some beer and wine but as my trolley was somewhat full (for the hungry hoard) I put the beer and the wine into the bags. I half expected alarms to go off and to be surrounded by surly security men (some customers I'm sure would like this but not me) but nothing happened. Of course, I was honest and took them out at the checkout but I bet many don't and I suspect they just walk through the checkout without paying. Can it really be that easy? I must check out checkout security sometime and report back. I looked again in vain for English wine this week without success. I thought someone of note (Mr King perhaps?) was reading this diary but perhaps not as Sainsbury's still prefer to stock horrible wines like Liebfraumilch and Piesporter (Pissporter, more like) in preference to our own home grown stuff, but there you go. Anyway, I did buy some Mouton Cadet at 25% off, so all was well. This is made/brewed/trodden by Chateau Mouton Rothschild in the Bordeaux region of France. The real stuff is unbelievably expensive (and red) but the people's offering of Mouton Cadet is pretty good. Did you know that each year a famous artist is commissioned to design the label for the Chateau Mouton Rothschild posh stuff? Picasso, Warhol, Kandinsky, Bacon et al. Interesting! Anyway, my daughter asked for some low fat olive oil (isn't this an oxymoron?) and I searched high and low for it. I have to say that there is a bewildering display of olive oils (or is it olives oil?) with some bizarre names – I noted Picual, Hojiblanca and Kalamata to name but a few. These are either the olive variety or where they come from, I can't remember, but, whatever, good for Sainsbury's on some clear food labelling for once. And if they can do it with olive oil, then why not the ready meals I ask myself? Now, one thing I found hard to resist was the Dyson animal hoover. This is a hoover that, bizarrely, is designed to pick up animal hairs but quite why one was for sale in my Sainsbury's I have no idea. Clearly no-one else does too as even with £110 (yes, £110) off it was still sitting forlornly on the shelves. Frankly I can't see it being there much longer and I expect it will go the way of the duvets, plates, wooden boxes etc in due course. I'll keep an eye on it and let you know. On to the checkout. I got in the queue for aisle 20 (it was busy today) quite near to the lectern (I presume this always comes out at busy times, like today lunchtime) and I heard the lecturer (he who mans the lectern) say "John (or somesuch name)

… 21 please". Aha, I thought if I hang back I can be first into aisle 21 and out quicker. Anyway, John (or whoever) eventually turns up and logs on and fiddles with the cash drawer and all the usual kind of timewasting stuff and by the time he was ready I had had to put my stuff on the aisle 20 receiving area (not sure of the technical name for this). Damn! My cunning plan has been foiled! Anyway, it was worth going through this aisle as the cashier turned the moving belt on without being asked (the first time in ages) and then kindly asked if I preferred it on or off. "On please" I said - absence makes the heart grow fonder! And she nearly got the Kids Vouchers right (£68 should get me 6 but I got 7) but why she got it wrong I'm not sure as I've just noticed that for the first time there is a Kids Vouchers bit on the bottom of the bill which tells the cashier precisely how many to give out. Maybe they are deliberately ignoring this and giving out as a many vouchers as possible? And if they are, good for them! And on that (belt) moving note that's it for this week (I hope – two visits are more than enough …). Sorry, not quite it, I've thought of another slogan for the Coinstar machine - how about "Relieve pressure on your groin, get rid of all that coin". No? Well, give me some credit for trying …

Items bought 39
Cost £68.49
Average cost per item £1.75
Checkout number 20
Nectar Points 1198
Active Kids vouchers 32 (still no e-mails asking for these!)

TUESDAY 17 APRIL - COHO MEMO

Lots to talk about this week, so here goes! We have had the vernal equivalent of an Indian summer over the past week or so and the temperature outside is in the 70s. So, ever mindful of the environment Sainsbury's have turned on their air conditioning and, my goodness, it is super cold in the area with all the fridges. Must remember to wear my arctic clothing next time! Anyway, on to the shopping. Whilst shivering in the vegetable area I noticed a little sign under the small clear plastic bags that you put your loose vegetables in (incidentally when these are scanned in at the checkout out they come up as 'Parsnips Loo' or 'Bananas Loo' on the little screen above the cashier. Hopefully not a reflection on the quality of the produce) that says they are 'recyclable'. Oh yes? I cannot believe that if these go to landfill they would take anything less than 1000 years to biodegrade and I suspect what Sainsbury's mean is that you can use them again, which is hardly recyclable in the usual sense of the word. I wonder who I can ask about this - I know I'll e-mail the big orange (the Sainsbury equivalent of the big apple) and put the question to them. I'll keep you posted! Now, at the cheese and ham counter I am referred to as 'Sir' by the ladies that serve (bizarre, I know, but then I am of a certain age) and today was no exception – "Thank you, Sir" said Mary or whatever her name was (should have checked, I'm slipping). Coincidentally, immediately after I had finished my purchasing, a young lady asked if she could take one of the small 'recyclable' bags at the side of the counter (them again!) to which the reply was "Of course, love". Love? It must be an age thing. I'm sure a lady of a certain age would be referred to as "Madam" as I am as "Sir" but below that age it's "Love" for all! One for you linguistics experts to get your teeth into. There was a big row near the sausages this week. Little Johnny had been sent off by his Mum to buy a stamp and had come back with a book of 12! Much lecturing from Mum about "Why didn't you buy just one?" (answer - the queue where they sell them was too long) and "£5, that's your pocket money gone for a week" (answer - pursed lower lip). He looked most disconsolate, poor lad, and if I had had £4.08 (the cost of 12 stamps, her math is worse than mine) I would have bought the book off them to relieve the misery. I use quite a lot of stamps so they would have come in handy. Actually it would have been only £3.74 as they would have kept one, but even for this lower amount I didn't have enough change on me. So I had to leave this forlorn little group to continue with their angst and soul searching. I did see them later on and relationships had thawed somewhat (moving out of the fridge area would have helped) as there was some more normal conversation and even the hint of a smile! Remember the Dyson animal hoovers and my prediction that they would be extinct within a week? There are now 4!!! They must be procreating after the store closes. I still cannot believe these will sell, but, then again, you never know - we are a nation of dog lovers. This week I saw an attractive young lady in a wheelchair doing her shopping with her basket on her knees. I watched her for a while (journalistic interest only) and as she had no assistance 50% of Sainsbury's products were simply out of her reach. This raises an interesting point about Sainsbury's policy for disabled access - no problem with getting into the store (plenty of lifts, wide aisles and so on) but when in the store then what happens? I wonder if Sainsbury's provide a helper if they are asked? And do they ask this routinely like they ask if you want help with your packing every time you go through the checkout? Of course, I should have asked her how it all works but when I thought of this I was pretty much finished and she had disappeared. Maybe one week I should feign disablement (à la Andy Pipkin) and see how I get on? On to the checkouts. No No 24 again this week - I am not hopeful of ever getting through this one as the aisle has a couple of broken chairs in it and the bit where you stick your shopping has piles of magazines & newspapers on it, so clearly it is seen as a bit of a dumping ground and not a real checkout. This week my cashier had a routine that I'd not seen before - she put certain items in smaller bags (those 'recylcable' bags again) before I stopped her. I assume it was something to do with putting smelly stuff (fish, dishwasher powder etc) in its own bags so as not to taint the rest of the stuff but, my goodness, is it really necessary? Has the world gone completely bagging mad? I asked for some petrol vouchers (as I said I would) and the cashier looked at me blankly which I took to mean "Sorry, Sir, petrol is not on a promotion at present". Or perhaps "Sorry, love, petrol ..." Whilst in the queue I did some interesting reading. When I released my trolley from captivity in it was a page from an internal Sainsbury's e-mail headed 'Plinth Update'. This seems to be some kind of stock control edict from the big orange as the first item was JS Wild Alaskan Salmon (which I had bought ...) and saying that 'We currently have excess stock of this line and are expected to incur significant wastage' and going on to tell my store what to do about it, in this case to reduce the price (now I could have thought of that) and to 'dress this product into the meat plinth in the space allocated for Young's salmon fillet promotion'. Not sure why fish is in a meat plinth and what is a plinth anyway? And won't Youngs be a bit cheesed (fished) off if they find they've been booted out? The memo went through all sorts of products - Cathedral City, jumbo king prawns, even champagne! Some were having their promotions extended and some were late with delivery from suppliers and so on. And each one had detailed instructions as to what to do and a name and London telephone number to call in case of query. So, presumably Sainsbury's have an army of stock controllers in London who are micro-managing each product in each store. Wow! I have to say I was hugely impressed. I thought I was organised but this takes this biscuit (metaphorically speaking, of course). In fact I am so impressed that as anything else would be a complete anti-climax I'm finishing this dairy entry immedi

Items bought 25
Cost £42.87
Average cost per item £1.71
Checkout number 20
Nectar Points 1282 (I feel a cashing in coming on)
Active Kids vouchers 29

THURSDAY 19 APRIL - TRICKY QUICKIE

I've had to return to Sainsbury's only 2 days after my last visit due to figure conscious daughter demanding copious quantities of salad! Actually I'm the kind of person whose cup is always half full rather than half empty so I'm using this mini-shopping trip as an excuse to go through one of the '10 items or less' checkouts and thereby claim another scalp. Disappointingly, though, I don't know which I've already been through so it's all down to chance. The excitement of it all (not). When I arrived, though, I found I didn't have my wallet so I was on a strict budget of £5.59 (all the change I had in my pocket). This required me to add up my purchases as I went along and not forget the totals, which I found difficult as I was being constantly distracted by all the activity going on around me. Anyway, I got it away as you will read (not much) later! Although it was a very short trip I noticed some ready meals with a notice saying that the tray in which they are packaged bio-degrades at the same speed as a banana. This is very interesting - if these meals can be packaged in a truly environmentally friendly piece of packaging, then why not everything else? However, I was somewhat suspicious as the picture of the tray in the notice didn't look like the tray in which the meals were packaged. Anyway, it's worth looking into more closely so more on this in due course. Also, my daughter kindly (?) pointed out that the Wheel of Health (or whatever it is called, I can't remember) on my quiche lorraine (or Lorraine Quiche as she is known on my bill - the well known French tart) is predominantly red, ie it's a killer. Perhaps it should be renamed the Wheel of Death for this particular product. Anyway she has challenged me to buy a much healthier quiche in future (if that's possible). I'll let you know how I get on. Finishing on a high note I went through aisle 3 at the checkouts - another notch on my trolley! And only spent £4.93!!

Items bought 7
Cost £4.93
Average cost per item £0.70
Checkout number 3
Nectar Points 1282 (as last time, didn't have my card)
Active Kids vouchers 29

WEDNESDAY 25 APRIL - THE WHEEL OF DEATH

Peace at last! The Godwin brood have all returned whence they came so I can get back to what I do best - shopping for one. Quite a bit to talk about this week so here goes ... First, I committed the cardinalest sin (not sure cardinalest is a word, but you know what I mean) - I bought a takeaway sandwich. Normally I don't buy these as I think they are ridiculously expensive for what they are but I spotted a cheese and onion sandwich and just had to have it for my lunch. And very nice it was too! Next, I took a closer look at the ready meal the tray for which is supposed to bio-degrade at the same speed as a banana. On the packaging there was a green triangle with a line through it and '7 Other' beneath it. Whatever does that mean? Luckily the stocker upper was in the vicinity so I asked him what it was all about. He was very polite and chatty but didn't have a clue either. He looked for the notice that I saw last week (he put it up) but it was nowhere to be found. So, I did a bit more research (internet) and I have found out that there are 7 green triangles (you guessed it, each on has a different number from 1 to 7 in the middle) with initials beneath them. They are all for different types of plastic - for example, 1 is polyethylene terephthalate (fizzy drinks bottles to you and me), 5 is polypropylene (margarine tubs) and 7 is ... other! 'Other' is defined as 'Any other plastics that do not fall into any of the above categories - an example is melamine, which is often used in plastic plates and cups'. It goes on to say that 'although presence of the symbol implies that the plastic item is recyclable, the symbol is actually only intended to identify the plastic resin from which the item was made'. So that's alright then? Well, no, actually because I am none the wiser about what I am supposed to do with this banana like tray in order to recycle it responsibly. I guess it would go in the general dustbin (which I think goes to landfill) which doesn't sound particularly responsible but as it supposedly has the biodegradability (how about that for a word) of a banana presumably in a few months there will be nothing left of it. Why is all this so bloody complicated? Surely there must be a more simple way of telling people what to do in an easy to understand way? Finally on the subject of recycling for this week, I did e-mail Sainsbury's about their recyclable small plastic bags and I am now waiting for a reply. Next, the Wheel of Health. You will recall that I was told off by my daughter for buying a quiche with 4 reds and 1 orange in the Wheel of Health (or Wheel of Death in this case). So, mindful of her advice, this week I sought out a healthier quiche. Bit of an oxymoron I know but, believe it or not, I found one. It was a Mediterranean Style Vegetable Quiche (not sure what Mediterranean Style means - full of water perhaps?) and it had 4 oranges and (yippee) 1 green. In the basket it went and whilst it was more healthy (or less unhealthy) than my usual quiche I have to say it was pretty grim. Clearly health comes at a cost in taste. Anyway, having saved some reds on my quiche I then bought a coffee cake which had 4 reds and 1 orange. My goodness, this must be the worst thing ever - I wonder if it is possible to buy anything with 5 reds??? But it was great! A child in a trolley said hello to me today. I think I should point out that Sainsbury's are not selling children

(Active Kids vouchers take on a new sinister meaning?) but he (or she) was in that seat type thing in his (or her) mum's trolley. Ever polite I replied "Hello" in a Mr Bean type voice, much to the child's amazement. Excitedly, he (or she) then proceeded to tell his (or her) mum that "That man said hello to me". Needless to say I quickly looked away and moved on - one can be arrested for that kind of thing these days. Next, cheese. The cheese and ham counter sells loose cheese (what a surprise!) and I took a note of the price of Cathedral City (£7.45 per kilogram) with a view to checking it with the packed price later on in the orangery. This I duly did - the packed price is £7.65 per kilogram. As I buy about 1/2 a kilogram at a time buying it packed is costing me an extra 10p. Well, even though 10p is 10p, as there is usually a queue for the cheese and ham counter I don't think that 10p is too bad an extra price to pay for not having to queue. Not sure of the equivalent hourly rate but still worth it I think. Well, that's about it for this week other than to tell you that I spent £35 today and was therefore entitled to 3 Active Kids vouchers but was given ... 18! So, I've now got 47 and if I was a school I could exchange these for ... nothing! I had a quick look at the catalogue and I can nearly afford a pair of Stampabouts (56 vouchers). These are upside down flowerpot type things with rope on that kids stand on and then walk with pulling the rope upwards as they go. So, in a couple of weeks time the first school to e-mail me asking for my vouchers could be the proud owner of a pair of Stampabouts! Wot, no e-mails yet?

Items bought 23
Cost £35.28
Average cost per item £1.53
Checkout number 11
Nectar Points 1404 (gained an extra 52 from somewhere)
Active Kids vouchers 47

Nearly the last one ...

TUESDAY 1 MAY - COME ON TIM!

Well, for the first time in ages the car park barriers weren't working. The entry barrier was up but so used are we all to the last few months of uninterrupted foreplay (pushing the button, waiting for a ticket etc) that, like fools, we all stopped at where the barrier ought to have been and pushed the button, waited for a ticket etc etc. I normally tend to drive in on autopilot, savouring the experience to come, but this broken routine woke me up and I noticed that the surface of the car park ramp continues to deteriorate. It is now quite bad although with the dry weather it's not a problem but when the rains come (in July, probably) the slipping and sliding will start all over again. Anyway, into the store. We get a good class of customer in 'our Sainsbury's' and a man asked at the cheese & ham counter where he could find water chestnuts. Good question! The ladies behind the counter (Carol & Marilyn) had obviously called for help from higher up the organisation because as I drew up with my trolley one of them said "This **man** needs help finding water chestnuts". Now, you will recall that I was called "Sir" a couple of weeks ago and a young lady was called "Love" so C & M were about evens on the politeness stakes. But, even so, this has marked them down quite heavily I'm afraid as they should have referred to him as a 'gentleman', I believe, to be technically correct. Doesn't politeness come before godliness? And whatever is a water chestnut anyway?! Moving on, there was a suspicious looking man (certainly not a gentleman) hovering near the bakery plinths (note I am now using the right word following the 'leaked' e-mail I found). And closer inspection of his name badge revealed ... the dreaded TalkTalk! My goodness just when I thought we were rid of the scourge for ever back they come. Anyway, unfortunately for him and fortunately for us he was not so much TalkTalk but SilenceSilence! I hung around looking at the rolls, cakes, doughnuts etc hoping he would approach me as I was interested in his opening line, but it was not to be. After a while people started to eye me suspiciously so it was time to move on. I looked back a couple of times but he was doing very little TalkTalking - no bonus for him this week. Not much else really happened this week - the 4 animal hoovers are still there waiting for a home - so it was all a bit dull but the checkout experience made up for it! I had the slightly unhinged cashier again this week (the one who, a few weeks ago, rather than turning on the moving belt with all the groceries on kept leaping out his chair and reaching round the corner to capture the next piece of grocery). His name is Tim! This week he was as animated as ever but much less physical as someone has told him about turning on the moving belt. He gave me a real scare though - as he scanned my wine he leant right across his till and looked me up and down and said "Are you 18?". "I was when I last looked" I said. Not a flicker, not a hint of a smile from Tim although the student in the queue behind me smirked. Now I was dreading the Active Kids voucher bit of the experience but he handled it really well – "Just over £40 so that's 4 vouchers plus 1 from the last customer" he said and gave me 5 (vouchers). He then wished me a happy first day of the month and I was on my way. Now before I close, those of you who are not mathematically challenged will have noticed that my Nectar points sums & calculations sometimes don't work. I think the reason for this is that some garages give Nectar points and if I'm asked if I collect them out comes my card as quick as a flash. That's the theory anyway but yesterday I 'earned' some points in a garage and my card was swiped but my opening balance on my Sainsbury's bill today was exactly the same as my closing balance last week, when it should have been higher by the garage points earned. Hmmmmm. Perhaps I need to check this out? I thought I'd done with Nectar points a few months ago but obviously not ...

Items bought 31
Cost £41.34
Average cost per item £1.33
Checkout number 14
Nectar Points 1486
Active Kids vouchers 59 (somehow I've got 7 more than I thought I had – even I can't count!)

TUESDAY 8 MAY - SAINSBURY'S HAS SOME FANS!

Some news first of all. I've decided to eat my freezers. No, this is not some kind of impressive party trick but I am fed up (not strictly true as I am shopping before lunch, but you know what I mean) with the scrunching as I vainly attempt to close the drawers which are overfull with bags, the contents of which are so coated in frost and ice that they are now unidentifiable. So, I am going to eat my way through the lot over the next few weeks so when she who is away returns we can start afresh. It will also mean I can defrost them (we have two, why I don't know it just means that there is twice as much space to fill with stuff we don't eat) without having to wrap everything in newspaper and put it into cool boxes and so on. So my weekly shopping bill at Sainsbury's is going to take a bit of a dive, sorry about that Mr King! Anyway, on to this week's experience. What first? The Top Ten Offers. I took a look at the board and noticed that Australian Cabinet Sauvignon is half price this week, reduced from £7.99 to £3.99. Now that's what I call an offer. Now, I'm never sure whether cabernet sauvignon is red or white. Between you and me I can't drink red wine as it affects my ears - after 3 bottles I can't hear. No, seriously, I used to suffer from tinnitus (ringing in the ears and red wine, gin, beer and so on made it worse) but, amazingly, I managed to rid myself of it (this is supposed to be impossible but I managed it) although I still steer clear of red wine, gin, beer etc. Is life worth living I hear you ask! Well, I'm still allowed white wine and lager so these I take in moderation. Anyway, I headed for the winery to look for a bottle but passing the fridge I spotted a white wine at half price so bought that instead. Summer has come to Sainsbury's! The store is littered with barbecue charcoal and, believe it or not, electric fans. These are all piled up in a corner waiting for nobody to buy them. I find it surprising that somebody, somewhere within Sainsbury's is charged with taking a punt on this kind of stuff on the off chance that it might sell. Personally, I can't see why Sainsbury's would want to take the risk - the chances are that most will remain unsold so why bother? Now the big question is - why won't they sell? Well, people come to this particular store to buy groceries and to my mind an electric fan is not the kind of thing you buy on impulse when your mind is set on broccoli, Special K, pork & egg cutting pie and so on. Also, I think there is a whole thing about being able to easily carry what you have bought to your car, on the bus etc and a fan in a big bulky box just doesn't pass this portability test. So, two reasons why I can't see the fans selling. We will see! Moving on to ... the savings card scheme. On the way out there is a machine with a notice on it encouraging customers to start saving today, on top of which are a pile of savings cards. Needless to say I picked one up. How it works is you stick a

£1 coin into the machine and you get a stamp which you stick on your card. How exciting is that! The card takes up to 25 stamps and you can redeem your card either wholly or partly completed at any store. It sounds like a complete waste of time, but I'm going to give it a go. I'll save up £1 for 5 weeks and then have a ceremonial cashing in – I'll let you know how it goes. On the way into the car park (jumping about a bit this week, sorry about that) I noticed that it said that the car park has 300 places. Now, I remember a few months back I parked right up the top in the last space just before you go into orbit and I have a feeling that the space was numbered although I don't think I noted the number in my diary (unusual, as this is the kind of banal fact that is meat & drink to me). When I go in next I'll don my space suit and go up there again to find out whether the car park does indeed have 300 spaces. I'll let you know. Anyway, that's about it for this week, but there's just time to tell you about the Half Price Deals leaflet. This is a glossy folded A3 sheet of paper in full colour showing all the ... half price deals. The place for these is, of course, as you come in but where did I find it? At the checkout! The local manager has this all wrong. What is the point of the Top Ten Offers board being half way round the store (next to the fish counter to be precise) and the Half Price Deals leaflet being at the checkout? These should be on prominent display near each of the doors as you come in - half way round and at the checkout is just too late as by then the average shopper has lost the will to live. This is always assuming that Sainsbury's want to sell their half price and Top Ten offers but, then again, maybe they don't ... That's it then for this week, until next time!

Items bought 18
Cost £26.37
Average cost per item £1.47
Checkout number 12
Nectar Points 1579 (gained 41 from somewhere - £20 or so of petrol?)
Active Kids vouchers 61 (I can now afford to buy a pair of Stampabouts, yippee!)

The penultimate one ...

OK, I know it's been 2 weeks or so since my last diary entry but I took the chance to go to France to 'visiter ma femme'. So, 2 weeks away from the orangery and has absence made my heart grow fonder? In a word, no! So, it is with a somewhat heavy unfondered heart that I make my first trip to Sainsbury's after returning. Actually, it turned out to be a really exciting visit but more of that later. First, I have noticed that the car park in which I park has won a ParkMark award. Whatever is this? Well, some research (internet) revealed that ParkMark awards are awarded (surprise, surprise) by the British Parking Association, an august body with a seemingly huge number of members. To join you have to have a proper car park (so my off-road parking space isn't quite enough it seems) or be a parking professional (basically any saddo with an interest in car parking such as planners, consultants etc). If you are any of these you pay £50 and you're in! You then get a specially trained Police Officer called an Accredited Assessor who comes along to your car park (does he or she park for free I wonder?) and assesses your car park against the 'Safer Parking Scheme Criteria'. Quite what these are is not disclosed but, anyway, if it's up to scratch you get a ParkMark award. What's in it for us users I hear you ask! Well the BPA website says that 'Park Mark awarded parking areas are run by responsible operators who are concerned with your safety and the safety of your vehicle, and who have done the best they can to reduce crime and the fear of crime on their site'. Well, frankly, I don't see it in 'my' car park. Although I will now specifically check I cannot see anything that makes it any different from any other multi-storey car park and if the operators are so concerned about safety how come the ramps going in and out continue to deteriorate at an alarming rate? I feel an e-mail coming on. Talking of e-mails I had a reply from Sainsbury's about the 'recyclable' clear bags used for vegetables and so on. It was clearly a cut & paste reply though as the font of "Dear Otto" was completely different to the body of the reply, which was disappointing, and it was, inevitably, full of the usual worthy statements but, to give S credit, it did answer my question. And the answer is that there are recycling points in their stores for plastic bags. Needless to say I looked for one today and there is a big orange (as opposed to Big Apple) plastic letter box type thing near the doors oozing bags from every orifice. I have to say I look at the doors a lot as I inch through the

the checkouts and I don't remember seeing this contraption before so maybe, after my e-mail, Sainsbury's had a big push to get them into all their stores? And of course there should be a big sign in the store telling us all what to do and how it all works - make it easy for us please! Now, on to the exciting bit. As I was buying my pork pie I noticed a small sign saying that if I was to buy 5 products with 'Enjoy Summer' stickers on I get a free cool bag or picnic rug. Needless to say I was really up for this and busily started to look for products with the sticker on. After a bit I realised that I must only buy things I would ordinarily buy otherwise I am, in effect, buying a cool bag or rug that I would never buy in a month of Sundays but in the end I managed it by buying 2 pasties, some (healthy) pâté, a quiche and 2 scotch eggs. Not very good on the Wheel of Health I admit but a rug is a rug! Anyway armed with this lot I get to the checkout leaving the 5 qualifying products till last and as the cashier finishes swiping, lasering, barcoding or whatever it's called I proudly ask how I get my rug. She looks at me as though I'm insane and I have to explain how it all works and show her my Famous Five and she looks at her screen and in the end calls over a supervisor who says I should have picked up a rug or cool bag from the piles in the store and then I have to wait while she goes and fetches one and I apologise to the tutting queue behind me and finally she comes back and the cashier books it through the till but then it won't automatically credit the £4.99 the rug costs so she has to do it manually and eventually it all works and I have my free rug! And very smart it looks too. Whilst all this was going on I noticed that the Active Kids promotion runs out in a couple of week's time and as no-one has yet e-mailed me for my vouchers I feel a trip to the local school coming on. Finally, I decided to start a savings card this week and I excitedly put my £1 coin in the machine and got out ... my £1 coin! So, I ask a supervisor what the problem is and she telephones the cash office who tell her that it has run out of stamps and the next delivery isn't until later. So, I leave the store to ... spend my £1.

Items bought 26
Cost £33.91
Average cost per item £1.30
Checkout number 14
Nectar Points 1645
Active Kids vouchers 64

The day after Bank Holiday Monday and it's pretty quiet so a leisurely shopping experience this week. What customers there were seemed to be in a queue at the ham & cheese counter. Ordinarily there are two servers so we are all dealt with in double quick time (the numbered ticket system never has to be used) but today because one of the servers was busy neatly putting out cakes and pastries on cardboard plates (presumably for a joining or leaving party?) we were left queuing & fuming. After a while of standing around I managed to catch the eye of the man who mans the fish counter (the Captain Bird's Eye lookalike) and, having pointed out the queue, within a few seconds we were overburdened with servers. Not a big deal, but it was frustrating that the server was more interested in some behind the scenes activity (the mind boggles) than in serving. Moving on, the dreaded TalkTalk representative was back in the store today. Readers will recall that the one before the last (the last one didn't talk at all despite me hanging around expectantly) asked me "Do you mind if I asked you a question?", to which I cleverly replied "Yes, but I won't reply". This one had a different script. First she asked "Do you collect Nectar points?". Red rag to a bull but, being an honest sort of chap, I answered in the affirmative. She then asked "Do you have a BT landline?" again to which I answered in the affirmative. I was then bombarded with if this then that we guarantee to save you 55% no contract blah blah blah. Too much information! I put up my hands in submission, shook my head and walked on. God, how I hate these phone companies, please leave us alone! I must be thankful for small mercies as they've nearly stopped calling me at home, thank goodness. My tactic of just putting the phone down and leaving them to chat on to nobody and eventually realising that I'm not listening and then trying to ring off which they can't do for about 5 minutes as my phone is off the hook during which time it's cost them money and they are unable to call yet more hapless buggers like me is obviously working. Anyway, on to the checkout and hurrah Sainsbury's have introduced a recyclable bag. It is much more sturdy than the thin plastic ones of old and people are encouraged to re-use them. Hmmmm. I'm not at all sure this will work as if people didn't re-use the thin flimsy ones why should they re-use the slightly thicker ones? Doesn't apply to me, of course, as I bring my green ones in every week. There needs to be an incentive –

why not deduct 5p from the bill of anyone who re-uses a bag and donate the money to environmental projects? In this way customers get paid to re-use the bags and Sainsbury's can be overtly seen to be an environmentally friendly organisation. Win, win! Having gone through the checkout I tried again to buy a savings stamp but again the machine returned my £1. I will give this one more go next week and then complain. Now, I'm doing this diary entry a few days after my visit (my standards are slipping) and I can report that there was a disaster with the wine that I bought. As I was drawing the cork (I think this is the right expression) the glass neck parted leaving bits of glass all over the place and in the wine. So, down the sink it all went and I vowed to return the bottle to Sainsbury's at my next visit. I know it was 50% off, but that shouldn't mean substandard bottles!

Items bought 32
Cost £53.25
Average cost per item £1.66
Checkout number 15
Nectar Points 1751
Active Kids vouchers 69

MONDAY 5 JUNE - STARS IN MY EYES

Well, I did what I said I would do and took my broken wine bottle back. The (senior) gentleman behind the enquiry counter freely admitted that he had not come across this before but was incredibly helpful and cheerfully returned my £3.99. He had to input it all to the computer and was a bit stumped over 'Reason for Return' but after a bit of discussion we agreed that 'Damaged' was as good a reason as any. He said that the bottle will be returned to the supplier for investigation, I wonder if it will? Perhaps I should e-mail Sainsbury's in London to tell them that a broken bottle is on its way. Talking of e-mailing Sainsbury's I have just asked them another question. On my Cheese & Spring Onion sandwich (naughty but nice) there are 2 asterisks after the price but for the life of me I cannot see on the packaging what this means. I see that * means 'From cow's milk' but ** is a mystery - so I've had to send another e-mail to Sainsbury's I'm afraid. I'll let you know what transpires. Today I had my second wonky trolley since starting my Year at Sainsbury's. Not bad! Mind you, this was incredibly wonky with a complete mind of its own so I have to admit it was a bit of a trial getting round without seriously injuring my fellow customers. I had a very short shopping list this week (not quite sure why, I have been eating normally) so I wasn't in the store very long and, as a result, there isn't much to report. At the checkout there was a big notice stuck to the till saying that there has been some impropriety with regard to Coinstar vouchers and that cashiers have to be wary. You will recall that the Coinstar 'turns coins into cash' (a bizarre slogan, but there you are). Unfortunately I didn't get time to read all the notice so I'm not sure what's been going on but it did remind me that I have yet to use the Coinstar, which I will do next week. Success! I put £1 into the savings stamp machine and got out ... a savings stamp. It's a funny little thing with 'Sainsbury's', '£1' and a reference number on it and a thin metal strip down the left hand side, presumably some kind of security device. Anyway I've stuck it on my card (this is all too exciting for words) and I think I'll get another 4 and then cash them in. It should be interesting to see how it is all handled as I can't believe anybody but me is doing this. Interestingly the gum tasted very odd, a Basics product perhaps? The Kids Vouchers have finished (boo hoo) and as no-one has e-mailed me asking for my vouchers I will donate all 69 of them to the primary school down the road. And that's about it for this week, short and sharp!

Items bought 22
Cost £26.97
Average cost per item £1.22
Checkout number 19
Nectar Points 1803
Active Kids vouchers 69

SUNDAY 10 JUNE - COINING IT IN

A Sunday visit this week - daughter now home from university and my fridge is somewhat short of produce and what there is lacking in quality (no salad, freshly squeezed orange juice - you know the kind of thing). It's busy and I have to admit that the cool of the fridge area is wonderful after the humid heat of outside. How did we survive without air conditioning? Now, first, I had a reply from Sainsbury's about the asterisks on my cheese sandwich. Again this was in two different fonts with my question repeated back to me in one and the answer in another. I presume that the advisor (or whatever they are called at Sainsbury's) cut and pasted the answer bit from another e-mail or document, hence the two different fonts. Anyway, the answer is that "the asterisks are a code that our supplier uses to help them with traceability and in knowing who made the sandwich". So, somewhere out there is a sandwich maker who supplies someone else who in turn supplies Sainsbury's. Literally a food chain! Clearly there can't be too many cheese sandwich makers otherwise the label would be covered in asterisks - more stars than the Milky Way. So, whoever ** is, well done, I enjoyed it. On the way in I had a go on the Coinstar as I said I would and it is a seriously impressive bit of kit. You chuck all your coins into a tray and it wheezes and clatters and clanks as it counts your coins and a little display screen tells you how it's getting on, it lists all the coin denominations and the numbers move up as your coins are counted. It also rejected a couple of Euro coins (20 cents?) that look very similar to our 1p. Great! It took its 7% service charge and out came a ticket for £1.30 for me to use at the checkout. Presumably Coinstar make money out of these machines but they must have to take in a huge amount of coinage to cover the cost of the machine, servicing it, taking out all the coins and banking them and so on. Anyway, good luck to them and I will return! Also on the way in I bought another savings stamp (£2 and counting) and stuck it on my card when I got home. All completely pointless really but it could be interesting when I cash it in as I suspect it will be a new experience for Tim or whichever cashier I get that week. Reader(s) will remember that I bought some summer offer products a few weeks ago so I could get a free picnic rug (which I've still not used). I have resisted the temptation to get another but noticed this week that the box which houses all the goodies has taken a real beating - clearly this offer is too good to miss and customers are falling over themselves to grab the rugs etc from the box before they all disappear. Nothing much caught my eye as I was going round the store but the checkout delivered for my diary as usual. First, the cashier picked up some of the next customer's stuff by accident and included it on my bill so this resulted in a crediting routine. Second, my Coinstar voucher caused some scratching of heads but it all worked in the end. Maybe I should save up a pile of this kind of thing and ceremoniously present them to a cashier all in one go? If I had enough of them presumably I could end up with a negative bill and get money from Sainsbury's! The ultimate achievement - being paid to do the shopping ... Third (is there no end to this excitement?) the man in front of me asked for help with his packing. Not sure why, he looked able bodied enough and fully aware of his surroundings but, anyway, I was expecting an onrush of orange coated assistants from behind the scenes but alas ... no. All that happened was the cashier picked up a carrier bag and stuffed his shopping into it after it had been swiped. Another illusion shattered! Finally, for this week I jotted down 'card' as I was going round but in the cold light of day I can't for the life of me remember why. Finally, finally, another interestingly described item on my bill this week - wild rocket leaves. An Iranian missile perhaps? And finally, finally, finally I did donate my Active Kids Vouchers to the school down the road and were they grateful? You betcha.

Items bought 27
Cost £38.49 (before my Coinstar voucher)
Average cost per item £1.42
Checkout number 8
Nectar Points 1877 (my Coinstar voucher cost me 2 Nectar points!)
Active Kids vouchers 0 (I will delete this bit next week)

WEDNESDAY 13 JUNE - NUMBERS GAME

Readers will recall that I recently spotted a sign going into the car park claiming that it has 300 spaces. Well, today I checked this out and ... it doesn't. When you get to Level 5 there is a sign forbidding you to go onto levels 6 & 7 (these are outside on the roof) but I snuck onto level 6 OK without being arrested or photographed but Level 7 has a gate across it so level 6 is as high as you can go. The spaces on level 6 are numbered from 253 to 295, so if this level was open for parking then the '300 spaces' claim would be fine but as it isn't, it isn't. So, clearly the car park owner is having trouble with his math. And he is having trouble with its spelling as well because the sign next to the door to the lifts (no escalators this high!) says that Sainsbury's customers need to validate 'there' tickets before leaving the car park. So, no good at numbers and no good at words - I feel a letter coming on! Going into the store a bizarre thing happened. I had just released my trolley (the last one in the trolley park) when a man older than me (yes, there are some) asked if I would stick my chainy thing into his socket so he could get his £ back. Now I assumed he had finished his shopping and as the trolley bay was empty this was the only way he could get his £ back so I agreed, stuck my thing into his socket (sounds painful!) and out came his £. So far so good, but the way these things & sockets work meant that I now had his trolley locked to mine. So, we had to reverse the whole thing and I referred him to the long chain in the trolley park specifically designed for getting a £ back when the park is empty only to find rather than leaving and going home he followed me into the store with his trolley. Maybe this is the Sainsbury's equivalent of "Do you come here often"? Moving rapidly on, I bought yet another cheese & onion sandwich with ** next to the price (the maker, you will recall) and, whilst making my selection, I noticed that ** makes other sandwiches for Sainsbury's as well. I wonder who ** is? And it is somewhat strange that there is no # or *** or even +++ so I can only assume that there are only two sandwich makers for Sainsbury's - ** and one other. I'm not sure I've got to the bottom of this yet - I feel another e-mail coming on after a bit more research. I decided to buy some healthy crisps (a real oxymoron) to go with my sandwich and alighted on some 'Salsa with Mesquite Kettle Chips'. Good grief, what on earth are these? 'Salsa' is Spanish for 'sauce' and 'Mesquite' is a either suburb of Dallas or a 'leguminous plant of the Prosopis genus found in Northern Mexico'. I don't go with the suburb of Dallas so presumably it's something to do with the Mexican plant, but what? The Kettle Chips website (yes, there is one!) is completely unhelpful as all it says is that 'Mesquite is the special ingredient which makes this tomato recipe intriguingly smoky', whatever that means. And where does a kettle come in? I've seen some gobbledegooky names for stuff in my time but this takes the biscuit. I think what they mean is 'Smoky Tomato Sauce Flavoured Crisps' but it doesn't have the same ring to it does it? Moving on ... it's checkout time! The re-usable bags have disappeared (Why? They were a really good idea) and our old friends the 'made from 33% recycled materials' bags are back. So Sainsbury's are still, in effect, advertising the fact that their bags are made from 67% non-recycled materials, which, frankly, is nothing to be proud of. Is it possible to make bags from 100% recycled material perhaps? If so, please let me (and Sainsbury's) know. On the way out of the store I was attacked by two Axa salesmen (unlike the TalkTalk salesmen the Axa lads hunt in packs). They were very polite, I have to say, but I was having none of it.

Items bought 27
Cost £42.78
Average cost per item £1.58
Checkout number 21 (only 24 to go now!)
Nectar Points 1961

SATURDAY 23 JUNE - WORST FIRST AID?

I've been 'en France' again so it's been 10 days since my last trip to Sainsbury's. There's quite a bit to talk about this week so here goes. First, on the way in I had to avoid a Virgin Media stall that had sprung up since my last visit. Luckily they were talking to a potential customer (mug) so I managed to slip by unnoticed. Second, I made a deliberate attempt to see if I could find a Sainsbury's product with 5 reds on the Wheel of Death. I'd already worked out that prepared pies and cakes were likely candidates and I was right! The Melton Mowbray Pork Pies and the chicken pies and steak pies were all 4 reds and an orange, as were the Viennese Whirls but I couldn't find anything with 5 reds. I wonder if there is anything? If you find something let me know please. Perhaps next week I should look for 5 greens - now surely that must be impossible unless it was bottled water or lettuce or something like that? Talking of greens, in the vegetable area I alighted upon a 'pointed cabbage' and indeed it was. I've never seen these before, if it wasn't in the organic range I'd be accusing of Sainsbury's of trying to sell us genetically modified vegetables. Of course, as everyone knows, the real name for these is 'Brassica Oleracea L. var. Capitata' and apparently they originate from some cross breeding in Germany in the late 20th century. Gulp! Doesn't this have a sinister ring to it? Whatever, I guess the ultimate in genetic modification would be cubed cabbages (ie cabbages in the shape of a cube) as these would pack perfectly into boxes with no air and wouldn't roll about on the shelves generally making a nuisance of themselves. Next, over the meat counter there was a banner with 'Best of British' on it. Now, as you know, I'm worried about Sainsbury's' use of the word 'British' so I took a closer look. The chops and other meat on the left of the counter had 'Produced in UK' on their labels whereas the Scottish beef had 'Origin UK' on it. My goodness, this sounds fishy (or meaty perhaps?). I have an awful sneaking feeling that the 'Produced in UK' is not British meat at all but has had something minor done to it in the UK so that Sainsbury's can say 'Produced in the UK'. I've e-mailed Customer Services about this – I'll let you know the outcome. If it does indeed turn out not to be British meat at all I will be apopeltic, aplotetic ... very cross! Anyway, I mustn't jump the gun but I'm not holding my breath. Now, here's a bit of useless information for you. Justin King (Mr King to you and I) drives a Maserati according to the Sunday Times. There is clearly money to be made in running a shop! I guess this explains why he has yet to visit my local Sainsbury's - it would probably get stuck going over all the bumps and humps in the car park and despite the ParkMark award I bet somebody would do some mischief to it. Don't be put off though Mr King - you can always park at my place and we'll get the bus down. Now, checkout 24. Regular readers will know that this the only real checkout (ie not baskets only, 10 items or less) that I haven't been through and recently there has been all manner of junk on it and by it - a broken chair, piles of magazines etc etc. Well, today it was clear and looking every inch like a checkout waiting to be used! I'll keep my fingers crossed although there isn't long to go now, probably only 5 or 6 visits what with my holidays coming up and so on. Great excitement whilst I was in the checkout queue. Over the public address there came an announcement 'First Aiders to the checkouts please' (I must admit I don't recall hearing public address announcements before, perhaps this is something new?). I looked up and down the checkouts expecting to see someone suffering from shock at seeing the bill or finding that a Nectar card had been left behind or some other serious ailment but it wasn't until I'd left the store that I spotted the culprit (or perhaps I mean patient?). A young girl was sitting on one of the benches looking very pale and sipping water with 3 First Aiders giving her helpful advice like 'Don't try and move'. Now, I'm not an expert in First Aid but "Don't try and move" doesn't seem particularly helpful to me, although I'm sure the Aider was doing his best. Actually I'm surprised that Sainsbury's can provide any form of First Aid under Health & Safety legislation because if, in fact, the worst thing this girl could have done was **not** move then Sainsbury's could well have been liable? Interesting. Or perhaps not. Anyway, the moral is – don't get ill in Sainsbury's, hold on a bit longer and go round the corner to Boots and get ill there, preferably next to the pharmacy counter. So, that's pretty much it for this week, other than to tell you that during my time off from Sainsbury's (for good behaviour) I bought some petrol and claimed some Nectar points with the result that the closing balance on my last Sainsbury's bill of 1961 points turned into an opening balance of 1991 points on this bill. Now, on the basis of 2 points for every £ spent this means I bought £15 of petrol but I thought I bought more than this? I really ought to check it out but you'll be pleased to know I've 'moved on' from Nectar points.

Items bought 23
Cost £34.74
Average cost per item £1.51
Checkout number 21
Nectar Points 2059 (another 30 from somewhere)

FRIDAY 29 JUNE - PRESENT EXPENSE

Well, I'm off to collect my wife from France demain (tomorrow) and will be gone for 2 weeks so this is just a quick trip to JS to say goodbye (adieu) and to pick up a few essentials like the presents needed for the French chums she has made whilst she has been away. My daughter is back home from university and amazingly she agrees to come with me to help! First, I introduce her to the Coinstar machine. It duly does its stuff with all the 1ps

I've been saving up over the last few months, spits out the odd non British coin and produces a voucher for £1.73. Daughter pronounces it 'cool' - praise indeed! We then march into the store proper and start to work through our list. After a while we realise that we need a basket so back I have to go to the entrance. Not my usual efficient self I admit but apart from this it all goes remarkably smoothly. We are greatly cheered by the fact that Pimms is being sold for £8 (yes, eight pounds) off per bottle - now that's what I call a sale. Shows the mark up though doesn't it as I presume Sainsbury's still make a handsome profit even with £8 off. As we have '10 items or less' we went through one of the '10 items or less' checkout and that was that. Easy!

Items bought 11
Cost £24.28
Average cost per item £2.20
Checkout number 6
Nectar Points 2107

SUNDAY 15 JULY - BRITISH? RUBBISH!

Well, my wife has now returned and here we both are doing a 'big shop' as the fridge and cupboards are bare. And whilst I am no longer a bachelor again (yippee) it does mean that, sadly, my Year at Sainsbury's is drawing to a close and with it my diary. But let's not be downhearted, it's business as usual for a few weeks anyway. So, what happened this week? Well, first, there is a new promotion – 'Swipe to Win'. Whilst this sounds like a prize for the person who can pinch the most stuff without being caught it is in fact a Nectar card promotion - if you spend more that £10 at Sainsbury's and present your Nectar card (hence the 'swipe') you get a game card. So, I duly get one but despite the upbeat '1 in 3's a winner' when I peel off the front the disappointing message 'Have Another Go' is revealed. This involves going on to the Nectar website (yes, there is one), typing in the unique code from my game card, then my Nectar number and then my e-mail address and then there is a load of small print that tells me that I have now agreed to be bombarded with 'offers' from Nectar (spam in other words). Luckily I have defunct e-mail address that I never look at for this kind of thing. Anyway having done all that I then have a choice of 4 balloons to pop (why is this all so difficult?) - I choose the green one and, surprise, surprise I am indeed a 'winner'. And my prize? £8 off horrifically expensive family attractions such as Chessington Zoo and Madame Tussauds. No doubt the other balloons have exactly the same 'prizes' and all of this is an elaborate way of collecting up e-mail addresses for 'marketing' purposes. Well, I won't be logging on to the Nectar website again but hopefully soon I will win first time and will be able to report a more satisfying winning experience before my diary closes. Talking of being caught for pinching stuff there was a security man from Reliance patrolling around this week (aren't they the lot that let all the prisoners go?). Is this a new phenomenon or have I not noticed him before? Perhaps he only comes out on a Sunday? Whatever, I presume he is there to deter shoplifters but I cannot imagine a young lad in a uniform wandering around looking bored is going to make any difference but I guess it's worth a try. But it did remind me to look for cameras! I'll look round a bit more carefully next time but I think there is definitely a hidden one above the drinks aisle as there is a suspicious odd looking circular thing in the ceiling above which I bet lurks a camera. Moving on, you will recall I was unhappy with the 'Best of British' banner above the meat counter when most of the meat had been 'Produced in the UK' according to its labels as opposed to it being 'Sourced in the UK'. Well I e-mailed Sainsbury's about this and my fears were well founded as they told me that 'meat that is produced in the UK means that the animal was not born, raised and culled in the United Kingdom'. So, despite the impression given by the banner the vast majority of the meat beneath it was British it was in fact **not** British. I am appalled! And whilst I am sure that Sainsbury's are following the rules it is quite clear the rules need to be changed. Not sure who is responsible for this (is it the dreaded EU I wonder?) but somebody, somewhere needs to sort it out. And it is blindingly simple! To be labelled as British the product needs to originally come from the UK. Period. Ignore all the processing, packaging and so on it's where the product originally comes from that matters. Luckily the banner has been taken down otherwise there would have been hell to pay. Anyway, on to the checkouts and a new experience this week! The cashier actually started a conversation. She asked me whether it was still raining to which I responded "Yes". Not a great conversation I admit but it's a start ... Next week I will make a point of engaging my cashier in stimulating conversation such as "Have you had your holidays yet?" (the good old hairdresser's favourite) and I'll let you know what transpires. Well, that's about it for this week other than to tell you that just like I said they would the Dyson animal hoovers have gone. I doubt they sold so presumably they have been rounded up and deported to Malaysia from whence they came.

Items bought 62
Cost £96.79
Cost per item £1.56
Checkout number 20
Nectar Points 2339 (another 40 from somewhere)

WEDNESDAY 18 JULY - SEND IN THE CLOWNS

Despite a 'big shop' a couple of days ago I've been sent back again for some more healthy foodstuffs - lettuce, yogurt, you know the kind of thing. On the way there was a traffic jam caused by ... a Sainsbury's lorry! I have to say I thought that big lorries were banned from towns during the day so quite why this one was on the loose at 4 o'clock in the afternoon I'm not sure. Anyway, its driver was adept at weaving his way through very tight spaces and in view of my (unhealthy) interest in Sainsbury's I was quite content to sit and watch him do his stuff (unlike the other drivers) leaving only inches to spare. Anyway, on to my shopping experience. Having bought the greenery on my list I passed the meat counter and noticed a bizarre sign which read 'Mey Selections'. I asked whether this was a spelling mistake for 2 month old meat only to be told that Mey is in Scotland and that this was an advert for the 'Sourced in Scotland' meat. Well, I've never heard of Mey, but on checking I find that it is indeed in Scotland between Thurso and John o'Groats, in other words in the middle of nowhere. I don't think there is much there apart from a castle, so it seems a bit odd for Sainsbury's to be including it in its advertising, although full marks for being absolutely honest about where the Scottish meat in fact is coming from (unlike the 'British' meat I had a go about last time). At the checkout the man in front of me had his face painted like a clown's and I was very tempted to ask him why but I'm afraid that I was wary of doing this just in case he was a little challenged in the brain department (you can't be too careful these days). So I asked the cashier instead after he'd gone, which gave me an excuse to engage in conversation with the cashier which I thought I would try and do from now on. Anyway, it turned out that he had a good reason for looking like he did (other than lunacy) - his daughter's party or something like that. Whilst in the queue I noticed a small child **under** the Coinstar machine! I presume he was looking for coins that had broken loose but I heard no whooping or cheering so I assume he was unlucky. On the way up the escalator without steps (I think this is called a travelator) I saw an old friend, an acquaintance really, coming down and we started a conversation that got louder and louder as we got further and further apart. She's the first person I've seen that I've known on my JS trips for ages - perhaps there will be more in the weeks to come on the buses principle that you wait ages for one to come along and then three come together. We will see.

Items bought 10
Cost £14.26
Cost per item £1.42 (didn't need a calculator this time!)
Checkout number 7
Nectar Points 2377 (including 10 free extra points, not had these before ...)

TUESDAY 25 JULY - SWIPE GRIPE

Coming out of the lift this week a man came in pushing a trolley and looking at the buttons who asked me, in a semi-hysterical voice, if there was a floor 2 and, if so, how on earth could he get there? Readers who've been with me since the start will recall that I had this problem early on so it's good to know that I am not the only geographically challenged shopper. I was tempted to let him suffer but took pity on him and told that he needed to take the lift to level 3 and then walk down the ramp to level 2. My good deed for the day! Also on the way in (is there no end to this excitement) I met someone else I knew. I bet there'll be another soon I thought, thereby proving the 'buses come along in threes' theory for humans as well. In the store I decide to buy another cheese & onion sandwich for my lunch only to find that they are no longer made by **. They are now made by . Whoever   is now seems to make all the Sainsbury's sandwiches so well done them for getting one over on **. No doubt at the ** factory, when they heard the news that Sainsbury's were taking their business elsewhere, all you could hear was **** and *******! Moving on, I took a good look round for cameras this week and I can report that there are none apart from the brown glass thingy over the drinks aisle. So, it seems that it is relatively easy to shoplift in 'my' Sainsbury's! I know that shops measure their shrinkage (theft) and it would be interesting to know how much is lost from 'my' store. I suspect a lot. At the checkout I noticed that the wobbly card wipe machines on stalks have been fixed so they are no longer wobbly. I commented on this in my diary ages ago so maybe somebody is reading it after all. I remarked on the stiffening (of the machines on stalks) to the cashier in the hope that it would result in some stimulating conversation, but it was not to be. And guess what! In the checkout queue there was someone else I knew. QED. Actually, to be fair, I wasn't sure it was someone I knew and I wasn't prepared to say hello to a woman on her own without being absolutely sure - I could get arrested for that kind of thing these days. Anyway, I'm 99.9% certain I did know her so I claim her as my third scalp. Now, I spent more than £10 or whatever it was I needed to, but I didn't get my Nectar swipe card. I realised this on the way out but hadn't the heart (or, to be frank, the interest) to go back and make a scene. Next time I will try to remember to ask.

Items bought 27
Cost £33.20
Cost per item £1.22
Checkout number 17
Nectar Points 2461 (including 18 free extra points – some of my purchases had extra earning power!)

The last one!

Well, here I am again and when tomorrow comes (1 August) I will be in my last month of my Year at Sainsbury's. When it's all done whatever am I going to do? How about a Year at Waitrose or a Year at Tesco? I'm open to offers! Maybe I should get this published (if I can find anyone insane enough to take it on). Perhaps Sainsbury's would be interested? I'm sure they would take it all in good heart - if nothing else it must be the most comprehensive customer survey they have ever had or, indeed, are likely to get. I could see it this Christmas nestling next to the magazines at the checkout and being snapped up by shoppers as a stocking filler. And making me a fortune! I can dream. And then there's the film rights! A bit dull I must admit but it has to be better than Big Brother ... Anyway, on to this week's shop. First, David Baarda. "Who?" I hear you ask. Well, Dave (as I will call him) grows tomatoes for Sainsbury's all year round according to the huge sign above the vegetable aisle. And a good, honest grower he looks with his moustache and body warmer. Quite why he has to wear a body warmer if he can grow tomatoes all year round I'm not sure. Whatever, I looked closely at the tomato packaging to find that they come from Yorkshire so they must be Dave's. And an internet search reveals that Dave does indeed run a tomato business on Teesside. Now, there's been a lot in the press recently about the floods and the effect on food prices and Sainsbury's have started to warm us up to this by posting a notice saying that some vegetables are in short supply as a result of 'harvesting difficulties'. Must be the understatement of the year! It will be interesting to see whether S puts up another notice in due course to tell us that their prices have gone up as a result of the 'harvesting difficulties'. Somehow I doubt it ... Next, small chickens. Regular readers will recall that many months ago I asked how all Sainsbury's small chickens can always weigh exactly the same amount week in week out, without any real conclusion other than to suspect skullduggery. Anyway, I haven't bought one for ages but this week chicken was on my list again and I noticed that the small chickens had 'New' stickers on them and that the price has gone up. Quite how they can be new as they've always been there I'm not sure but there you go. And I have no problem with the new price as it still seems ridiculously cheap but ... yes, you guessed it, they are still all exactly the same weight and price. If anybody knows the answer as to how this can be please let me know asap as my diary will be closing soon. Whilst passing the cheese & ham counter I noticed that the pork & egg cutting pie is back. It is, however, following the return of 'elle' from France no longer allowed so, tempted as I was, I had to pass it by. Whilst in the queue for the checkout I noticed a couple pouring huge quantities of coins into the Coinstar machine much to the interest of everyone in the store. Money laundering perhaps?? This week I remembered to ask for a Nectar game card only to be told that Sainsbury's have run out. How can this be? I thought of lodging a complaint but decided against it - if they have still run out next week I will though. You have been warned!

Items bought 29
Cost £49.55
Cost per item £1.70
Checkout number 10
Nectar Points 2559

FRIDAY 10 AUGUST - IN GO MY PENNIES OUT COMES £10!

It's been a while since my last visit because I've been given time off for good behaviour. Anyway, as I zoom into my last month of my diary there is still much to report. First, today there was a big banner up over the door saying 'Over 7000 prices reduced since January'. This is an interesting statement as I presume this means that in 7 months 7000 items have been reduced in price for a period of time before being increased in price (ie the Top Ten special offer and the like) rather than there are 7000 items in the store that are cheaper than they were at the beginning of the year. This has got me wondering how many items there actually are in the store? There would have to be more than 7000 but how many more? I might do a bit of math & calculation on this before the end of August - it would be nice to conclude with a wonderful piece of research. Despite the grotty weather the 'Enjoy Summer' promotion is still in full swing - the box containing the picnic rugs, cool bags, badminton kits etc is full to overflowing and is even more battered that it was a couple of weeks ago so presumably people are still fighting over the goodies. My picnic rug is being used this week by daughter – I'll report how it fared being sat on by 3 'young ladies' and having assorted liquids and solids spilt (or is it spilled?) on it. And just when I thought we were safe the animal hoovers are back, only 2 of them so there has clearly been a cull but back nonetheless. Will they be still there, looking forlorn, as my diary closes in a few weeks time? The excitement of it all! Next, the Coinstar machine. I took in a huge pile of pennies & twopences (and other assorted buttons, Euros and the like as it turned out) and was reward with a voucher for £10.36. My goodness me it did make a noise as all this lot was processed and the nearby checkouts ground to a halt as the source of all this racket was sought and then stared at. I stood there nonchalantly whistling (as you do) not caring one jot and watching the counter click up the 1ps, 2ps 5ps etc etc. Finally on this quick visit - rocket. I jotted this down but now cannot for the life of me remember what it was all about! Ah well, perhaps it will come back to me and if it does I'll let you know.

Items bought 15
Cost £23.05
Cost per item £1.53
Checkout number 18
Nectar Points 2605

MONDAY 13 AUGUST – PRICES AND DEVICES

Well, I knew it wouldn't last and here I am back again 3 days later. Looking on the positive side it means you are getting your money's worth as my diary nears its conclusion. So what happened today? Well, I noticed that there are lots of little stickers up all over the place saying 'Tesco price check' and then an amount which is exactly the same price as the Sainsbury's price. I can't see the point of this. OK, so some stuff is the same price as Tesco is but statistically that has to be true for a certain percentage of what Sainsbury's and Tesco sell given the large number of items that arc the same in both stores. So why tell us? Actually it begs the question as to which items are more expensive in Sainsbury's and which are less expensive. Perhaps what Sainsbury's should do is to put little stickers on items that are cheaper than in Tesco – assuming, of course, that there are some. Is this allowed under competition law, health & safety rules etc etc? Probably not ... Moving on to a subject dear to my heart - wine! Sainsbury's put the white wine that is 'on offer' in a fridge near the drinks aisle and as I was extracting a couple of half price wines I noticed a little sticker (this is my week for stickers) saying that 'To maintain great prices fitted with security device'. Whatever does this mean? First, there was no security device that I could see and what fitting security devices has to do with great prices I really don't know. The only thing I can thing of is that security devices prevent theft and theft costs money so less theft means cheaper prices. Maybe I'll e-mail Sainsbury's and ask them - but, then again, perhaps not. Some excitement at the checkout today. First, the man in front of me spotted that his orange juice was leaking so there was the ringing of the bell which was followed by the going and getting another one routine. And then it was the wrong one - he wanted one with bits in. Men have to look out for their bits! So then there was another ringing of the bell followed by the going and getting another (correct) one routine. Success! By now the queue was building up nicely. And then my cashier had trouble with finding my nectarines on his fruit price list. There was much looking up and down the list and scratching of head and in the end he asked me to find it for him. This I duly did with no trouble (if you're interested nectarines have the code 4063). By this time the queue was snaking away into the distance and I fully expected the lectern that comes out when it's busy to be rolled out for an emergency consultation. Whilst all this was going on I noticed a book tucked behind the till with the title 'Record of Challenges and Refusals Book'. I assume this is for noting instances when people under 18 try and buy drink and the cashiers are unable to 'Cashier Confirmed Over 18' having looked at passports, driving licences and the like. Is it a legal requirement? And what is in it? Is it Big Brother at work again? I must take a peek and report back! The title of the tome is interesting - surely 'Record of ... ' is sufficient, without 'Book' at the end? Another one for Lynne Truss or John Humphrys. Also whilst in the queue the alarms went off - is there no end to this excitement? As ever they were completely ignored by everyone apart from me. Looking around for the reason (perhaps a 14 year old was trying to buy drink?) I noticed that there are 3 lights on the wall - red, amber and green and the amber one was flashing. It soon stopped but I wonder what the red and green lights are for. I ought to find out - if there is a real alarm I want to be first out! Finally today I met yet another person I knew on the down escalator as I was going up and out. Funny how I've been coming to Sainsbury's for a year and it's only in the final weeks that I've run into people I know. Where were they for the rest of the year? And finally, finally eons ago I said I would check out the 'Cashier Confirmed ... ' as sometimes my bill says 'Cashier Confirmed over 18' and sometimes it says 'Cashier Confirmed Over 16'. I'm on the case.

Items bought 29
Total cost £42.47
Cost per item £1.46
Checkout number 22
Nectar Points 2689

SATURDAY 18 AUGUST - LETTUCE AFFRAY

There was a great item on the news recently - a man had got more than he bargained for when he bought a pack of Sainsbury's lettuce as inside was ... a lizard! This caused much mirth on Radio 2 where I heard it (the station for people of a certain age). Anyway, it sounded a bit of a long story but in the end the lizard went to a reptile collector and Sainsbury's visited him and gave him a replacement bag of lettuce, which was very big of them I thought. Funnily enough, the day after I heard this, a squashed beetly looking thing (dead and cooked) dropped out of my Sainsbury's bread as I was cutting it. Ordinarily I would be straight back to the store with it but I decided that if all you get for a lizard in a bag of lettuce is ... a bag of lettuce it probably wasn't worth it. So the beetle went into my brown friend outside the front door (it's been promoted from the back door) to await turning into compost or whatever they do with the mush that is collected once a week. Anyway, onto this week's shop. Once again I met some people I knew on the up escalator as I was going down. Perhaps the people I know only come out in the summer? Now, these two are 'neighbours' who we don't speak to. They have built themselves an old people's bungalow at the bottom of our garden and lied and cheated their way to getting a building built that was never approved by the local Council in the first place. It's taken forever and we've had to endure planning appeals, the Local Government Ombudsman, worry, frustration etc and it's all cost us a fortune. Meanwhile Lord & Lady Muck sit in their garden sipping their Sanatogen as though nothing has happened. So I did the usual 'staring and ignoring' routine at them as they trundled up the escalator. Believe you me I will get my revenge and it will be so sweet! Into the store. I bought some blueberries this week. In truth, I've been buying them for a while since 'elle' has returned from France and I noticed that the price sticker has £3.99 crossed through, then £1.99 crossed through and finally the real price of £1.49. As far as I can remember this has always been the case so it seems the illusion that we are getting a bargain is just that - the price always has been £1.49 and perhaps this is a ploy to make us thing that we are getting something on the cheap. Another e-mail to Sainsbury's perhaps? Success! You will remember that I found a product with 4 reds and 1 orange on the wheel of death (health) and surmised that it would not be possible to find a product with 5 greens unless it was water? Well, this week I did indeed find a product with 5 greens – 'British Chicken Quick Cook Breast Steaks'. Needless to say I bought some immediately - a British product with 5 greens, how exciting is that! On to missing milk. As I turned into the milk area I saw two Sainsbury's lads hunched over a calculator type thing uttering words like "We should have 5 of these" and "Where can they have gone" etc etc. I chatted to one of them later on and I found out that Sainsbury's can scan the bar code of any product into this little machine and it tells them how much stock they have. So, if you know how much is in the stockroom you can then work out how much should be on the shelves. How clever. And even more clever is that most of the time what they should have, they have, although when there is a discrepancy it is usually less stock than there should be probably due to shrinkage (theft to you and me). And I'm not surprised that there is less milk than there should be as it is a Saturday and the light fingered brethren amongst us would have been hard at work. Next, the Top Ten items. As you know I often look at the Top Ten board and today was no exception. But guess what was on there - Bernard Matthews turkey! It seems so long ago that I was giving BM a hard time in my diary following the bird flu scandal (Bernard Matthews turkeys – they're flootiful) and I can't remember what the outcome was. Were they guilty or not guilty? Whatever, Sainsbury's are obviously still stocking his questionable turkey products and I'm delighted that it seems they are struggling to sell them and are having to put it on their Top Ten offers board to get them away. You will be pleased to hear I've stopped putting my vegetables into those clear little plastic bags and I now put them loose into my trolley. This gives me the opportunity to lay them out neatly on the checkout conveyor as though they are in a show waiting to be judged! I really must get out more. I was greatly excited by a banner offering 5p off petrol for the next few weeks but due to the excitement of the vegetable laying out I forgot to ask the cashier for my voucher. Damn, must remember next time. And next time or the time after may be the last of my Year at Sainsbury's ...

Items bought 29
Total cost £36.11
Cost per item £1.25
Checkout number 12
Nectar Points 2761

WEDNESDAY 29 AUGUST – I THINK IT'S ALL OVER ...

Well, this is it. The last entry in my 'A Year at Sainsbury's' diary. Not my last ever visit to Sainsbury's as life and shopping go on but certainly my last recorded visit! And how was it for me this week? Pretty much the same as usual. Going in, though, there was a cleaner ... in the car park. I'm not quite sure why anyone would want to bother to clean a car park, particularly this one as I don't recall ever seeing any rubbish, bottles, paper etc lying around during the last year as, if I had done, I would have beefed on about it ad nauseam in my diary. Perhaps the ParkMark subscription renewal is looming and the owner wants to spruce it all up ready for that all important police visit? Anyway, into the store. As I walked in I noticed the security man was 'giving me the eye'. Now I don't think I am the suspicious looking type but I guess anyone who has 2 large green bags open in his or her trolley has to be a prime suspect. How easy it would be to drop a few items in on the way round and then not get them out again at checkout time? Well, not me, my friend, I don't do shoplifting. Readers will recall me asking why Sainsbury's had little stickers all over the place saying 'Tesco Price Check' and then a price which is exactly the same as theirs? I said that I thought it was a complete waste of time but today it did me proud. And why? Because doughnuts have gone down in price from 13p (or was it 12p?) to 10p, because the Tesco price is cheaper. So, I bought 2 to celebrate even though they are no longer allowed following 'le retour de France de ma femme' and the more healthy eating husband campaign that started within hours of the return. There was a bit of excitement in the bin bags area today. We have started using paper bags in our 'Mittelstation', these are quite expensive to buy and so I had them on my Sainsbury's list. For the life of me I couldn't see them and in the end I asked one of the assistants if she could help. Now, this assistant turned out to be a rep for Korbond and she was only there to stock up the Korbond display stand. Korbond? They sell sewing stuff and they have a small concession in my Sainsbury's store. I wonder how much that costs? It can't be very much and I'm surprised Sainsbury's bother with it as presumably they have to do all the math at the end of each month and send Korbond a cheque for how much of their stuff has been sold. Anyway, back to my paper bags which in the end it turned out that Sainsbury's don't sell. Sorry, you're probably still wondering whatever is a 'Mittelstation'! Well, our brown friend outside the front door (it's been promoted from the back door) is called the 'Brunesheisehause' and even if you can't speak German I'm sure you get the drift. And my daughter (who, incidentally, reported back favourably on the free rug) called the caddy (to give it its technical name) the 'Mittlestation' as its half way from the plate to the 'Brunesheisehause' – it's a sort of skiing term as on long cable car journeys there is usually a changing over point half way up which is called the 'Mittelstation'. Get it? Probably not, but it's as good a name as any. You'll be pleased to know that I've investigated the 'Think 21 Cashier Confirmed Over 18' line that appears most weeks on my bill. It's all pretty obvious really as it shows on my bills just above any entry for alcoholic purchases – presumably it shows on the cashier's screen after it's gone across the beeper to remind the cashier to check that the customer looks over 18 (not difficult in my case). And I've been able to sort out why when I bought the Sunday Times last September my bill said 'Think 21

Cashier Confirmed Over 16'. Do you have to be over 16 to buy a Sunday paper from Sainsbury's? And the answer is … sometimes. Apparently on occasions some of the material in a newspaper may be a bit 'racy' and so there is an age warning on it. Well, I could understand this with the News of the World which is full of filth (so I'm told) but the Sunday Times??!!. Unfortunately it is so long ago now that the particular paper has long gone so we will never know. Now I said a couple of weeks ago that I would try and work out how many lines Sainsbury's have in their store. Well, this week I did and the answer is 24,362. Impressive, huh? Well, I counted the number of items on an average looking shelf (plinth?), multiplied this by the number of shelves to give the number on one side of the aisle, then multiplied by 2 to give the number per aisle, then multiplied this by the number of aisles and it came to somewhere between 20,000 and 25,000 and 24,362 is as good a number as any. As I got to the checkouts I looked wistfully at aisle 24, the one that has eluded me all these weeks, but no luck, it is still being used as a sort if dumping ground. Disappointing that I couldn't get a full set but I didn't do too badly, did I? And, as it is my last week, I cashed in 2500 Nectar points and my savings stamps and my Nectar vouchers. I didn't tell you about these did I? On my board in the kitchen with post it notes, calendar, useful telephone numbers etc I found 8 vouchers worth 500 points each (God knows where they came from) and I waited until my last week to cash them in. And what a result! All this lot added up to a massive £37.50, meaning that my bill was reduced from £64.14 to £26.64. If I'd thought about it I would have engineered it so that the deductions were more than the original bill meaning that, in theory, Sainsbury's would have owed me money. And then waited to see what chaos ensued. It's easy to be wise after the event! So that's about it. But before I go, some statistics. Over the past 12 months my My Sainsbury's bills totalled a massive £2,816 from which cashed in Nectar points worth £30 were deducted (equivalent to a 1.06% discount) resulting in a net spend of £2,786. I bought I hope Mr King appreciates my custom as if it wasn't for people like me going into his store week in, week out Sainsbury's wouldn't be what it is today and he wouldn't be driving his Maserati. And is Sainsbury's in good order? Actually, I think it is. It's organised, cleanish, good value (I think) and the staff I have talked to over the year (sometimes asking them the most bizarre of questions) have been helpful and courteous. There are things I would change, for sure, and maybe one day my diary will find its way on to Mr King's desk and he will get them sorted. And have I enjoyed my year? Well, I'm not sure 'enjoyed' can ever be used to describe grocery shopping but I've certainly found it interesting and I've learned a lot. But I can't finish without a final word about the checkouts! I never did get through 24 but managed all the other real ones. Here's how I did:

Checkout	Visits	Checkout	Visits
7	2	16	4
8	4	17	2
9	2	18	3
10	2	19	2
11	4	20	5
12	4	21	2
13	3	22	3
14	6	23	2
15	4	24	0

So well done 14! Finally, I'd like to say a big thank you to all of you readers who have stuck with me over the weeks and months – now you can 'try something different today'! And with that I am going to close my diary for the last time with the words used by our beloved leader (Blair not King) when he stepped down … "That's it. The End".

Items bought 44
Total cost £64.14 (before £32.50 of Nectar vouchers and savings stamps)
Cost per item £1.45
Checkout number 20
Nectar Points 323 (after cashing in 2500)

'I always say, keep a diary and some day it'll keep you'

Mae West

'Let's hope so'

Otto Godwin

Printed in Great Britain
by Amazon